Pandora's Box

Paperback Version

This book is a work of non-fiction. Unless otherwise noted, the author and the publisher make no explicit guarantees as to the accuracy of the information contained in this book.

© 2012 Ernest Johnson. All rights reserved.

No part of this book may be reproduced, stored in a retrieval system, or transmitted by any means without the written permission of the author.

First published 2012
Published 2012 by Karah Kious-McJoslin,
KarahbarkDesigns.com

Cover art by Karah Kious-McJoslin

ISBN: 978-0-9882803-6-6

Pandora's Box 1
CON MANS FORMULA 4
   GET-RICH-QUICK A PUBLIC WARNING 6
   DEEP INNER GAME - THE DRUGS INGREDIENTS 9
   HUMAN CONDITION 11
   MENTAL STIMULATION 13
   WHY WE BELIEVE IT 14
   YOU CAN DO IT 15
   MIND SET 17
   YOUR MISSION 18
CLOAK OF THE LIVING DEAD 20
   LIVING DEAD WORLD: 20
   LIVING DEAD J.O.B.: 21
   LIVING DEAD BODIES: 24
   LIVING DEAD FOODS: 24
   LIVING DEAD WATER: 27
   LIVING DEAD MEDICINE: 29
   LIVING DEAD RELATIONSHIPS: 32
   LIVING DEAD BELIEF: 35
   LIVING DEAD RELIGION: 38
THIRTEEN REASONS WHY YOU'RE SICK, BROKE &
DUMB 46
   MORTGAGE-HOME-BUYING 46
   LAND 46
   DEPRECIATION 47
   MANUFACTURED HOUSING 48
   MOBILE HOMES AND LOTS 48
   RENT 49
   EXPENSES 50
   J.O.B. 50
   LET'S RECAP 55
   TAXES 55
   DEFINITION OF TAXES 56
   GOVERNMENTS 57
   FOODS 58

WATER	60
DRUGS LEGAL & DRUGS ILLEGAL	63
THE LAW	65
YOUR TIME IS SPENT	67
MIND DISEASE	70
A WELDER AND HIS DISEASE	79
LONG TERM (CHRONIC) OVER EXPOSURE EFFECTS	81
LIST OF KNOWN DISEASE	90
LIST OF KNOWN SYMPTOMS	91
SKULL AND CROSS BONES	92
OVERCOMMING THE DISEASE	95
MY DARK QUEST	98
SHOCK AND HORROR	100
THE RESULT	101
A CURSED MAN	102
THE BLESSING	102
WHAT IS YOUR ASS WORTH	104
THE AMERICAN BITCH	104
MOMMY AS TEACHER	107
Woe-man	108
NEW AMERICAN BITCH	110
PROSTITUTION	110
BUSINESS WOMEN PROSTITUTES	116
QUEEN STATUS	117
About the Author	119

CON MANS FORMULA

Charlatan: One who cries out in the market place. Seller of papal indulgences. A person who pretends to have expert knowledge or skill that he or she does not have; fake; mountebank- SYN. Quack.

Charlatans are somewhat of a magnet. They are masters of illusions. They are masters at spinning a web of deceit. They will tell you a story using dynamic principles. Their success is dependant upon variables; mainly the gullibility of human nature. Charlatanism is a science that is fabricated blended with the natural to make it believable. Charlatanism is pure devilish in nature. It is a seduction.

In the old days a charlatan would place himself on a high wooden platform and commence an oratory to a crowd of people and bring them under a seductive spell. They would take an inspiration spin it in such a way using a mixture of truths and half truths that sounded consistent with reality. It was a very entertaining process. It took everybody out of their mundane lives and transported them into a fantasy.

Charlatans have a keen awareness for human nature. They understood how to attract a crowd and hold you in their spell. Once you are in their web you are easily seduced. What they had to say was what the people wanted to hear. To put it in simpler terms, the people came under a spell. I think it could be likened to a spiritual moment. Our lives are very mundane. This is why it is attractive.

Charlatans perfected the art of attracting and hold the attention of the crowd. They worked the crowd by reading them and adapting to their mood quickly. Once the crowd came under their spell, some people became followers. Once they had followers a cult like following could occur.

Their success depended upon a few factors; having a good game plan and your gullibility. Having something everybody wanted. Last but not least, their ability to cast you under their spell.

Today, they are called sales people. They use the same rules doing it just about the same way. Sales people are not the subject here. I have no raw feelings for anybody working in their official capacity.

Today's get rich quick is the spirit of the charlatan. They offer a product for your money so this does make it legal. But how they do it I consider unethical. They offer you the moon and the stars, but cannot deliver you a can of beans.

Charlatans then and now are masters of creating passion, zeal, and enthusiasm from the masses. It works so well everybody does it. People not only buy it but those who do it swear by it. In fact you can see that when you read their ad.

Being a charlatan did have a down side. Once the crowd got whiff of their scam they were run out of town. So they had to keep their bags packed. Game over. Over time their game got perfected.

If they were successful in swaying the crowd, the listener would come to their own conclusions. Their minds were taken into the clouds where things get hazy. The listener is stimulated into all kinds of dreams. Then the listener will see what they want to see. The imagination of the listener takes over and imagines infinite possibilities. The listener gets elevated to a higher plain of consciousness. This in turn brings good feelings. It can be transforming. It certainly is good entertaining.

Charlatans make their vagueness attractive. They use great words of resonance, but cloud their meaning. They use words and phrases full of heat and enthusiasm, fancy titles for simple things. They use the power of words and numbers. With this technique things become hazy and deceptive. All this creates an impression of specialized knowledge. This gives them a veneer of profundity, making it sound fresh, new, and exciting. They top it off with a guarantee. But it is only for 30 days. Not much time to do anything; yet so few understand it. I certainly didn't.

In the beginning of their seduction, the listener does not see is for what it is. Once you are duped by it too many times, you will eventually wake up to the game. It is a game you know.

There was never any reality to it. Nothing ever materialized for me, did it for you? Hoped deferred made my heart sick.

Charlatans create an aura about them selves. They build themselves up with lavish splendor. After all, what do you know about them really? Nothing, that's what. Our eyes see this and become fixated. It keeps us from seeing the ridiculousness their ideas and the holes in their belief system. It also attracts more attention. It appeals to our senses. They use theatrical effects and make us believe they have something extraordinary. They disguise the source of their income. They make their sale through the side door. Pretty cleaver isn't it?

GET-RICH-QUICK A PUBLIC WARNING

Before you invest in a get-rich-quick scam, a word of advice; have fun with it. Look at it as a creative investment. Chances are very probable you will not really gain anything form it except experience and a little knowledge. It is a learning curve. Don't expect too much. Use it as a tool for greater things. It is your school of hard knocks. It offers high expectations and delivers no results.

They all offer the secret to unlock the ability to lots of money. They all offer promises to a better future; and opulent life style. But so far none has delivered for me or anyone I know. The time has come for somebody to address this issue hard and cold. It's time to clear the air waves so to speak. It's appalling.

It is simply nothing short of predatory. They dangle a carrot in front of you and tell everything it isn't. It is alluring. They play with your intellect and your emotions. They know your human condition. They understand your condition in life and they are here to take advantage of it. Take advantage of your weaknesses. They prey upon your stupidity, your gullibility. They laugh at you all the way to the bank.

They might as well say; "Hey Stupid! Look at my scam; it is better than any other. Look how much money it has made me? I now live like a rock star. I guarantee you it works". But you have to pay me to find out. Thus, creating an illusion.

Illusion: A mocking; deceit; to mock; play with; a false idea or conception; an unreal.

You and I are out busting our buns in the real world, while they use trickery to make gain. These people have lazy asses. They are a breed of people that cannot face the truth about the reality in their lives. They are an inferior breed of low life. There is a growing class of humans that would rather stick there face in the sand than face the hard cold reality of things. They have no class, no skill, can't be competitive. So they stoop low to a diabolic level.

There are many diseases of the mind. This is one of them. They are con men pretending to be business people. In the con artist's arsenal of weapons are trickery, shrewdness, false promises, cleverness, deception, illusions, delusions, concealment, and cloaked in mystery. They lie smartly. They vaguely define. They are mysteriously evasive. They inspire you to their disease.

The lying, twisting of facts, fabricating, telling of stories, swindling, and stealing, are all upside down and back-word behavior. They operate in obscurity. Yes! This is a mind disease. But the amazing thing is that it works. It has no place in our future but yet it is here. It has no place in our now but it is here and now. It lives here in front of us all. We all see it and do nothing about it. Yet most of us are duped by it. I know I was and still am. It is like a drug. In the new world to come, they will be reduced to zero starting now.

In the new world to come not long from now, such behavior will not be tolerated. There will be no place for them. Such people will either get it straight or be banned. Only those who produce value will remain. All such people who cannot produce value will be singled out. This includes politicians from all levels of federal, state, and local levels. Embrace it.

We live in a world in which grace is under fire. Meaning that which is good is Thrown to the ground and called bad. That which is bad is now called good. The lines have been blurred.

It has been replaced with cleverness, deceit, illusions. They have made a mockery of all that is good. They have destroyed all that is natural in its wake. The get-rich-quick operates from fantasy. It is a made up story. It is make believe. Is there such a thing as a get rich quick? Sure, in your fantasy. Can it happen to you? Maybe so. How can you do it? Well, I can't tell you how. That's for you to figure out.

I will say this. Fantasies are healthy. That's why they work.

The creator of the program is the one who will be making the money. There is no easy anything. Nothing is really free. They will tell you anything you want to hear to get your money. You see, there is no secret to sell. They make their money scamming you out of yours. Question is can you do the same your self to others? Success favors the bold my friend.

They tell you all that you want to hear. No selling involved. Easy lazy cash. Stuff envelopes. Make thousands weekly, no experience required. Work anywhere. Work from home. All they are doing is recruiting dum-dums like you to help them in their quest with the promise of lots of cash but not for you.

Your vulnerability is being preyed upon; they feed you with a poison pill. Sure it sounds good, taste good but has no substance. It leaves us sick with desire. The essence of deception is distraction. Distracting the people you want to deceive gives you time and space to do something they won't notice. The act of kindness, honesty, and generosity are often the most powerful forms of distracting because it disarms peoples suspicions. It draws out there eagerness. A gift is the perfect object to hide a deceptive move.

Basically, it's a fabulous con job. It is truly a brilliant piece of art. It works because they have put aside their morals. They have no boundaries.

DEEP INNER GAME - THE DRUGS INGREDIENTS

What makes it work is a combination of a lot of things: Our human condition. Our over stimulated lives and the deterioration of all things. But the drugs ingredients are an essential part of its success. It is a formula actually. But we will call them the rules of engagement.

1. Conceal your intentions: There intention is to sell you something valuable, but can't tell you what it is. It is a secret. You must pay to play. But when you buy you find out it is worthless and through it in the trash. In the mean time hide your shame.
2. Make people come to you: You simply place an ad in some paper, some poor slob sees it and thinks there is an opportunity. He responds to your ad and you get paid. Since the respondent is some poor slob what is he going to do when he gets ripped off, get a lawyer?
3. Appeal to peoples self interest: Self interest meaning money. Their promise of easy money is a magnet to your self interest. Every one is greedy.
4. Pose as a friend, work as a con: They show you they are human and appear very friendly. They show human openness. There confidence is in the formula.
5. Keep everybody thinking: They tell you absolutely nothing. What they do tell you is everything it isn't. They do give you a convoluted list of what it is not. They do promise you the moon but you don't really get what they promised.
6. Play upon peoples need to believe: The need to get your bills paid is reason enough to believe. No need of convincing here. People have an inherent need to believe. Everyone has two hundred reasons to want to believe they can have it all.
7. Play with people's fantasies: Reality sucks. We all have a need to get out of reality. Fantasies are healthy.

That's why they work. Again, there is an inherent need already in place.
8. Work on their minds: Their program as a whole will work on your mind. As they take you into the clouds your mind will activate. This in turn plays tricks on your mind.
9. Act like royalty: Have you ever noticed they act like they are coming down off their high rolling ways to offer little ole you their one of a kind secret. Don't make sense does it?
10. Never appear perfect: This just shows the public that you are human. They almost always start their story line about their lives, and their struggle, and their discovery of their secret.
11. Preach the need to buy: but never give too much. They do preach the need to buy but will not give you anything concrete. That is why there is only 30 days guarantee. They can't give you too long or you will figure them out. Everything is fluid.
12. Make people dependant on you: Their story line always indicates that they have the one and only secret. You the sucker are in need of this easy way to lazy cash. This makes you feel you need them to get it. But you must pay to find out.
13. Use honesty and generosity selectively: They appear honest about their lives. They show generosity with their free reports. But this is about as far as it goes.
14. Know your audience: They are well aware of their audience and the condition or your life. They are in tune with peoples degraded human condition.
15. Master the art of timing: What this means is the form. The way it is all put together. How it is put from start to finish. In other words it is a controlled con. They have developed game.
16. Give before you take: Give something away for free to stimulate good feelings. This gets you loosened up.

The principle is as old as china. This tactic is disarming. After all, who can resist something for free.
17. Assume formlessness: This is a no brainer. Are they flighty or what. There is a lot more involved but you get the picture. The seduction process is a diabolic. It's an emotional magnet. The lure of money who can resist. They tap into fantasy. It brings out the child in all of us. They think their way inside your head.
18. The bold lie: Con artists know that the bolder the lie, the more convincing it becomes. The sheer audacity of the story makes it more credible, distracting attention from its inconsistencies.

HUMAN CONDITION

Our human condition is both better than you can want; and you are worse off than you think.

Every one wears a mask in society. We pretend to be more sure of ourselves than we are. We do not want other people to glimpse that doubting self within us. Our egos and personalities are much more fragile than they appear to be. They cover up feelings of confusion and emptiness. Because of this low state, we are susceptible to seduction. The seducer knows this. This is called a state of unreality.

While we are in this state of unreality we are vulnerable. In our vulnerable state of unreality we are weak and lack a sense of completeness, we feel something is missing inside. Nobody is completely whole. We are all divided beings yearning inside to be whole and complete. From deep inside we look outward to fulfillment. In us all is a constant groaning, anxiousness to be fulfilled. Our humdrum lives are filled with repetition, boredom, which leads to un-fulfillment. We are all hungry inside and have a deep desire for fulfillment.

Since the beginning of time in our human organism lies a basic need for love. This is called a primeval love, otherwise known as primal love. Where we do not get it, we there fore lack it. Most of us do not know what love is, not really. Therefore, were always looking for it in some way. Our daily routine are so filled with things and events of survival, it takes us away from it.

There is no such thing as a perfectly satisfied person. Everybody screams to be seduced. Everybody desires to be taken out of their bad reality and be led into some other fantasy. Or is it the other way around? Either way it's all mixed up. If you have satisfaction today tomorrow you may not. We live life daily.

We all feel tension and disharmony often enough. Stirs within us all are feelings of discontent and unhappiness with our circumstances and our selves. The reason being is because our life lacks adventure and we have gotten away from the child of our youth. You now live a boring life. Out of this boring existence come feelings of inadequacy and anxiety. You alone are responsible for your own life and feelings.

We are all complex and ambiguous, full of contradictory impulses. We all know what the truth is but are unwilling to come face to face with it. We live in a state of denial. We are lazy creatures. Let others do it. The truth hurts too much, it is too ugly, it is too inconvenient.

Lots of people are living in pain. Pain and anxiety are the proper precursors to pleasure. Pain is the low pleasure is the high.

Most people have great difficulty reconciling the person they are with the person they want to be. You have to drastically change your self image. All things old must go. Your personal appearance must become new.

What you really want is not just temptation but to give into temptation. To yield. It cost to much to resist than to yield. It is your nature to experience temptation, taste its forbidden fruit. It yearns to be satisfied and become whole.

Everyone has that one weakness. Everyone has that child like insecurity. Something they lack in their life. Everyone has a weakness for some forbidden fruit.

The whole world yearns to be seduced. The child in us all wants everything now, regardless of the consequences. The child in us all has little power to resist. A child lurks in everyone.

There are pleasures that have denied you. Your desires have been repressed. You are in tune with your own limitations. You have no understanding of the weakness of others around you.

We all struggle to keep order in our lives. It is very tiring on our person. We become exhausted. We all have our doubts and regrets about the things we should have done or the person we should have become. We have to always repress our strongest desire. It takes more energy to be virtuous and good.

In the end we are alone in our struggles. Our belief in God is put to the test daily in hundreds of ways. Every night we wish the devil would just get off our back. But we know the pleasures of the world are what bring us happiness, so we compromise. Most people's problems have complex roots; deep rooted neurosis interconnected social factors, roots that go way back in time and are exceedingly hard to unravel.

All of these factors are present and I haven't even mentioned drugs or alcohol, nor the medical issues or politics. All of the issues of the day are derived from the human mind disease. The mind disease can simply be defined as missing the natural mark.

MENTAL STIMULATION

Our minds have been over stimulated. Everyday we are bombarded with all kinds of mental stimulation, television, radio, work, and family. This is just the beginning. The point is we are over stimulated. Just one of these let alone two or more is enough. Many of us have children to raise. That alone is enough to send any parents mind into overtime. Stress baby, stress.

Now more than ever our minds are in a constant state of distraction. We are continually bombarded with endless information to digest. Pulled in every direction, we find it impossible to turn off our overactive minds. The attempt to shut out simply triggers more thoughts. What is needed is to shut down our thinking process and just be. But that is not so easy. So to slow it down we focus on one thing. This is our only escape. It slows the mental process down. The get rich quick is also a stimulant.

The get rich quick is an eye catcher, attention grabber. It offers all the things we desire. Life has made us dead, boring, and inattentive. Our jobs have no life in them. The make fast cash now quickens our spirit. Makes us come alive. All that our non-natural lives deplete from us, the making of lazy cash promises to replenish. It can be considered life giving. This is why we are attracted to it. Our over stimulated minds are bad on our libido. Making large sums can help fix that problem. We yearn for an end to all of this madness. It is insane.

To make matters worse the high cost of everything just keeps going in one direction. We all have deep debts. None of us are experts at finances. But our wallets are being raided. Everything in life demands our attention and our cash. The making of 500.00 a day flips this coin to the other side.

Our bills are endlessly frustrating. We are constantly distressed by them. Some are distraught, while others are feeling hopeless. We are always seeking to be relieved of them. To make a thousand a week would go a long way to alleviate this burden. That's why we are attracted to it.

The get rich quick is a system, it is an art. It is a seductive process. It is designed for human consumption. It promises infinite possibilities. But for many, it has been a disappointing experience.

WHY WE BELIEVE IT

First of all, we are uneducated in the diabolic nature of the get rich quick scam. Second of all, we need to believe in something. People are lazy by nature.

The masses want the lazy way out. The masses do not want the ugly truth. Getting it the right way takes too much. People secretly crave enigmas. People secretly love mysteries. People love fantasies. People love to be led. People need to be stimulated. It gives some poor souls hope.

To believe in it is likened to a life source. It can quicken the spirit. When your body is sickly, our minds are not well, bills increasing; the pressures of life getting to be too much, people will do just about anything to beat it. This is why we believe it.

The system is deteriorating slowly and we know it. We look for anything to make our lives better. Money makes the world go round. Money buys anything and everything.

The get rich quick is an emotional magnet for some, a money magnet. It pulls at them. It pulls at me. We know it must contain a certain level of deception, but we ignore it. It holds the power we crave. It defies all logic. It promises to restore all that has been lost. Our dignity, replenish our bank account. We will labor no more.

We will have financial power. Money will fulfill all our family's needs. We can live our fantasy life style. We will not have to face our ugly reality as we know it.

As human beings, we are not supposed to be living in squalor. The world has got us down. We have no way to look but up. Our backs are against the wall.

We are tired of working for the company. The company has no soul. It is unfeeling, and we are human. We become desperate. This is why we believe. We inherently sense that there is a better way out there.

So, reset your own personal price. Be the creator of your own program. Put somebody to work. Find your own niche in the world. Seek out your own value. Put it together. Give it to the world. You shall have it all. Do your own con game.

YOU CAN DO IT

Plant the seeds of your destiny. Your destiny lies within you and you alone. What are your gifts? What can you offer others that is of value? The duality of nature is ever present. Your ego will follow you. Put these two mind sets secondary. Find your silent witness. Yourself that simply is. This is primary.

Put away struggle, the wrestling with issues. What has it gained you? Know the difference between problems that need attention and those that don't. Why are you wasting time and energy on negatives?

Your biggest obstacles are your fear, your worries, and your doubt. These are the curses of mankind. They are the greatest destroyers of success. You must over come these insidious monsters; you cannot afford one negative thought.

Look to your supreme ambition. You have one. What is it you have to offer the world? Give birth to your dreams and desire. They want to be born. They want to be alive. Give your self to these things, and happiness will crown you. You are a mini creator. You were born to be the star in your life.

Poverty of character leads to poverty of life. Abundance of character leads to abundance of life. The earth is full of abundance. Look around you and see what it is you can do, not what you can't do.

You have internal boundaries, yet you have no boundaries. Figure that one out. Energy of will is a self originating force. Weak people wait for opportunities, strong people make them. Remember the three P's; patience, practice, perseverance. This means move forward with perseverance. Have patience along the way, and keep at the thing by practicing daily. All things come to those that practice this simply formula.

Successful lives do not come about as a result of chance, luck, or accident. Success is born out of applied knowledge and wisdom. We all have the power of choice. Make your choices count. Prepare your self to receive that which you earnestly desire. I can't never accomplished anything positive.

Have an over mastering idea, a single and intense purpose. Set a goal. Become obsessive about it. Take the opportunity to broaden, deepen, and heighten your horizons and your God given talents. Once you have an idea you must work for it, sleep for it, live and breath for it. Master it in all its detail. The laws of nature will aid you at every turn. In its own time success will crown you with glorious achievement. Those who get obsessed to their achievement will plow new horizons.

Fuse yourself with your dreams, your wants, and your fantasies. Make them your reality. Get rid of self imposed limitations. Find the switch in your being and flip it on. Renounce the belief that the world has power over you. Understand your boundaries. Don't waste your internal fuel. Go beyond the five senses. Have faith. Create a new beginning. Don't look back.

MIND SET

Disgust and discontent is your driving force. Determine to make your self more valuable to society. Do not settle for less. Look around you and see how others are doing it. Don't try to reinvent the wheel.

Wake up to a new reality. You have been conned into believing you are worth little. Embark on a new journey. Seek betterment. Increase your value. Reset your financial thermostat. Shake off the old mind set. Shift your priorities. Every cell must shift.

It will not take over night. Use time. Pay your dues. Expect more. Liken it to climbing a mountain. Leave everyone behind. Go it alone. Never mind the opinions of others. Be in charge of your own destiny. Shape it, form it, and mold it.

Invest in your self. Increase your skill set. Ask your self, why would any one follow me? Don't believe in your job. It will never bring you anything lasting. Stop at nothing to attain your goals. There are countless opportunities. Embrace who you can be. Learn skill sets.

It's all about value. Take stock in your resources. Only you can decide what your worth. Don't settle for less than what your expectations are. Look to what you can accomplish.

Your destiny lies buried in your bosom. In your desperation you will find a way. Only you can find a way. Only you can decide a direction. How bad do you want success? Are you willing to look deep within your self? Can you offer solutions to other peoples problems?

Elevate yourself. Know who you are. Deal with your fear. Dig into your emotions. Be yourself. Be relaxed. Disconnect from everything negative around you. Develop a new focus. Become the person people need. What does it take to rake in $50,000 a month? Figure how to do it. Become your product. Start with your dreams.

Market yourself out of the rat race. Everything is a trade off. Put your self in front of the public. Marketing is a variable for entrepreneurs. Marketing is moving the product. It is the vehicle. You must become a master marketer.

YOUR MISSION

What is your mission? Your mission has got to be not self centered. You must compromise. Think dollar signs. Stop focusing on your self. Focus on helping other people. What is your long term purpose? What is the big picture? Think wide scope.

Join a team or a marketing group that is on a mission to do something big. It's not about the money. It's about purpose. Light a flame in others. Everybody's mission is different. As you go forward your mission will unfold. Live your life by design.

Choose from a whole new world of opportunities. You can have anything you want. Your dreams are accomplished automatically by helping others. You are where you are by design. You have unrealized abilities.

Choose who you listen to. Throw off the old you. Create yourself anew. Live your own fantasy. Figure out what and who you are. Your mission should be bigger than you, big enough for others to follow. Can you be the leader others are looking for?

It's all about who you are being. What can you offer the world that's original? Success starts with passion for what you are doing. Be passionate not passive. Passion is inspiring. It is powerful energy. It will drive you forward.

Be obsessive to empowerment. Start with your hobby. Your mission is in ending the struggle. You have to be developing and growing. You have everything within you to succeed. It's about commitment.

What are your intentions? Develop ideas. Then stay focused. When will you take your business and your self seriously? Will you crash and burn. Are you willing to do what the masses are not willing to do? Can you be in the top three percent?

Find a mentor and coach. There is a 100% chance of success. Few people are willing to do what it takes, are you. Your life is now about fulfilling your mission. Quantify your mission. Where will you be in six months? Take responsibility for your mission. Figure out why you're here. What is it you want? Then go on a journey to attain it. Don't settle for less. Be authentic.

Have you ever in your life had a challenge that you did not rise to. Then later in life it reared its head again. That is your cue. Your new mission is calling you. Rise to the challenge, quit being so lazy.

Your life chart is ticking. The time is now. Do it now. The secret to life is to live in the moment. Make every moment count. This is the secret to happiness. Drop the unreal. Your inspirations need a mission. Give it birth. It yearns to be born. Once you give birth to it, nurture it, love it, become it. Use it or lose it. Your character is your destiny.

CLOAK OF THE LIVING DEAD

LIVING DEAD WORLD:

How can I explain this? I can count nine different ways on living death. Living death is non-living, it is existing only. It is a zombie like state while alive. It is numb. Not alive really. It is dumbed down. It is half awake and half asleep. Not aware of your surroundings. It is living with the veil over the eyes. Zombie means: A weird, eccentric, or unattractive person.

The medications you take and the mental state you have all the time produce in us a zombie like state. We are in a trance like meditation. We perform our daily functions in listlessness, mechanical like existence. In short it is what ever is not good for the living organism. The list listed above is just a sampling of what here is. But the things available to us are hideous. But they taste good. What a paradox.

We are a society that is really, really sick in every way. Just look around your self and what do you see? We have dead relationships that are pretty much a waste of time. But we continue in them. We have domestic violence on both sides of the coin but we stay in the relationship. What a joke. We have a world on its way to hell now this is a tragedy.

Tragedy: means, serious drama describing a conflict and having a sad end. This is indeed the state of affairs of most of our lives and the world.

We have chemically altered bodies, but nobody cares. We have dead end jobs that do nothing but pay our bills, nothing more. And then again they are becoming fewer and fewer. What a tragedy. What we have as a result is all manner of ill thinking and ill living. This too is an epidemic.

We are all walking zombies and don't realize it.

LIVING DEAD J.O.B.:

Tell me how do you like your job? Can you say that a little louder please! I didn't hear you. OH! That's what I thought. It's not to your liking, is it?

It simply doesn't go well with your living organism does it? I didn't think so. You're telling me. So tell me about it.

I live smack dab in the middle of the city with heavy traffic right outside my door. I see them all going to work everyday. I have not seen anyone go by yelling and hollering that life is fantastic this day or any day. It does not happen. You are to busy being a slave.

Talk about job, let me tell you a story about job. I had a job. Yes! I did work at one time. You bet I did. I have had more than one god damn job. I have had so many god damn jobs that I am highly qualified to sit here and tell you screw your god damn job. I was a believer just like your dumb ass. OH! Yes! You say Well! Smart ass tell me about you stupid job! OK! Sit your ass down and listen up! Here goes. Are you god damn ready?

I was a welder fabricator since 1977. How's that for starters. Can you guess where I am going with this? You guessed it. I trashed my body breathing those fumes. Not one employer ever freaking cared about any future condition. I have seen a lot of jobs since 1977. Not even my spouse can understand my eventual pain.

So my attitude about jobs and employers is not the same as yours. I have an entirely different point of view towards things. I am not an innocent little following lamb like I used to be.

What we have in our society are a bunch of little lambs that follow the bad shepherd. Hopefully you are not one of them.

I know your thinking, 'well you should have known better.' Truth is I did know, head knowledge that is. But now I know like I never knew before. I have had to learn to reverse this constant pain. I have had three conditions. I like to brag and say I beat them all. But the truth is you cannot reverse any thing one hundred percent. I did kick it in the ass though. I mean I beat it into submission. But not completely.

Saying that just to say this I do speak from experience. I know you can feel my aggression here, but let me tell you it is this aggression that I have that got me where I am today with my conditions. I am an over comer. I am a survivor. I will not put up with any disease in my body. I had to claim my body back, which means I had to fight for my health. My job just about killed me. I served it then it brought me diseases. After that My job kicked me to the curb in the name of age.

Now I cannot help but ponder all of my brothers out there who have made their living just as I. I feel for them humbly. At first I felt angry at all those around me because I had so much pain and they did not. But now I am in a much better place in my life that I can now ponder the fact that maybe I was one of the lucky ones. I have great empathy for all of my brothers and sisters who work in environments that are unhealthy for their bodies. So I know about job all too well.

I too believed in doing the right thing and getting myself a trade. I paid my dues in this category. This is the main reason I sit here writing this essay for others. I was a value producer. Now I have decided to become a value creator. Produce my own values. Become a self guided individual.

I pick my jobs carefully now. A couple employers know that I am a ticking time bomb. Am I feeling sorry for my self here? You bet! But I am over it now.

Tell me how do you like your job? Does it bring excitement to your life? I hope it does. But chances are it doesn't.

When I lived on large acreage we had a lot of sticker blackberry bushes. I mean we had them infested. I had my day at them. As God as my witness and the far away neighbors too. I have spent many an hour in the sticker patch. Have you ever spent time in the sticker patch? Well, I have and I can tell you it is a thorny affair. I have dug them up by the roots. Hugh roots that is. Digging up thorny blackberry bushes is god damn grunt work. But at the end of the day I would feel better and had worked harder than when I went to work on job. Working the ranch is the hardest work there is. But the job is the most stressful place to be. My true confession is this. I did enjoy the tough environment. It made me a mean bastard. Well, not a bastard per se. Just one tough mother fucker. I now view the city life gangsters as little boys that think they are tough.

They have no fucking idea what life can be. Some gangster kids just need a little smackin' to remind them of who they are and who they are not. Talk about smackin' I think a lot of people could use a little smackin'.

My point is simple. In my job I felt used and under appreciated, stressed out and tired. Job is full of bull shit.

Managers! Oh brother please do not get me started. They all sit around thinking of ways to dump their responsibilities onto the workers. On the ranch I could work all day at a much harder rate and love it. Even get more done in a ten hour period. One was good for my being and the other one was not.

Another thing here while I was on the ranch, I built myself a welding shop. I learned how to create all kinds of things. I have made my self iron benches, beds, gates, and metal sculptures. This was the best time of my life. I created valuable pieces of art. Now that was good for my organism. Again compared to job, job really sucks. These are pieces of art that will be with me for the rest of my life. I will view them later as proof.

So my view of job is that I now see right through it. I think the employers pick up on it now. That is why they hire younger ones. Well good for you. I know what it is they are looking for. I decide along the way if I will work for them and how much. They don't pay I walk. My mission now is to cause some chaos in my industry. Just for old time sake. It is my way of saying thank you for my disease. Jobs are for the living dead.

I put together a packet called a welders and the disease. I called it the skull and cross bones trade. If any one wants a copy, just ask and it will be there.

Are you having a good time yet? No! Well, let's continue.

LIVING DEAD BODIES:

Look around you and what do you see in the public domain. I see people who have bodies that are chemically altered. Need I say anything more here?

The chemically altered bodies are starting to happen at younger ages. I have a small son who is over weight at a very young age. He refuses to eat any fruits and vegetables.

I can't say this is his fault but it is a fact nevertheless. He likes and dislikes what he likes and dislikes. It is what is inside him. He is not at any fault. My point being is this is not natural. It is completely unnatural. I really have deep empathy for this child. But no matter how much I desire for him to eat healthy he will refuse it. So as a result his body is chemically altered in the present tense and will continue in the future tense. How did this happen? Well, over the past several generations we have been introducing more and more chemicals into our environment that we are currently in overload status. We have chemicals falling out of the skies for heavens sake. Like I said before, there is a plan in place to replace all that is natural with all synthetic.

Is there a conspiracy theory to make your body out of proportion? Of course not. I didn't say that did I? But Hey! If you think there is then share it with me please. What is the reason for this? I think the reason is stupidly simply. To keep you dumped down and unable to physically do any thing. It is to put you in a helpless state. This is just one aspect of dehumanizing. So that when you are led to the slaughter what can you do? Nothing, that's what. "So fatten up the stupid little lambs. For we shall harvest them
Soon" says the gods!

LIVING DEAD FOODS:

Box foods baby! Absolutely! Sprayed chemicals on our fruits and vegetables. They do not come off with regular water. The only way pesticides can come off of those fruits and vegetables is with 11.5 alkalized water. They do not come off any other way that I know of.

They want you to eat them verses organic because they have chemicals.

Our planet is loaded with mind and body altering chemicals. I heard it said that more than 70% of our foods in the typical grocery store are filled with chemicals. Is it any wonder people are walking around with altered bodies?

Reality is that our bodies are starving for nutrients and we don't know it.

I read a story once that went like this. There was a band of gypsies hundreds of years ago. They were a cruel lot. They kidnapped children and made them into dwarfs. They would kidnap very small children. Then they would put their bodies in a barrel, with only their head, feet, and hands sticking out. These poor children would live like this for years. At the right time they were released from this barrel prison. Guess what there little bodies would look like?

You guessed it. They were the shape of little barrels.

Hideous isn't it, cruel as well. Thoughtless!

Now as the story goes, there is a plan in place to do the same to you and I. Don't believe me. Well! Just look around you today and watch who is walking down the street. I see lots of people looking like they have lived in a barrel. Their bodies have been altered. Am I just seeing things? Can you see it too? Maybe not. I challenge you the next time you go into the public domain, look around you and you will notice them all over the place. A better place to find them is just go look into the mirror. Are you one of these people? If so, you can thank your local food distributor. These people are great at lying about things. In fact, I can bet you too are good at justifying things as to why you're the way you look. I can hear all of the excuses now. I'm not guilty of anything you say. Maybe not. But no one made you go to the store and eat the foods you eat.

No one put that ice cream in your mouth either. Did they? I rest my case.

Like I said before it is a paradox. We need foods. But then again the foods are the way they are.

Let me cover one base here before we go any further.

All of these said things that I have stated about or will state coming up does not belong in the right and wrong category. Nothing should be considered right or wrong. Right and wrong is vertical thinking. I some times refer to vertical for explanation purposes only. My view is no longer right and wrong duality. It is if it is good for my organism or not. Period, end of story. This leaves out religion, truth. It introduces wide scope honesty about the things that are. It is well known that we should eat foods that are closet to nature as possible. Fast foods and the western diet are known world wide as unhealthy. But the fact is they taste pretty good. In fact I eat them sometimes my damn self.

See! I know I am a hypocrite. Yes! I am. Sorry. But I am different, right! I had to fight to get my self to where I am today. Nothing is to be rejected in this world if you decide. I just watch my self and consider it a treat once in a while to eat out. We all think the same here. Your health is what is in question here. These foods are for the masses, therefore they are foods for the living dead. Yes! I too am the living dead that is why I know.

Sickness starts in an acidic body. Your poor little body cannot let these chemicals go. The body holds onto them because it does not know what to do with them. It does not know how to release them. So, these foreign matter stay in the body altering it. What is a body to do?

What goes in the body is just as important as to what doesn't get to go into the body. All foods are modified. They are boiled, fried, and most of the minerals are removed. Now your body has chemicals in it and then starved for what it really needs. This sounds like an evil plan to me. Is any body at fault? Can anybody be held accountable? Of course not.

My life time new motto is if it is green its good. This includes money, vegetables, and marigold.

What do these chemicals do for the body? Absolutely nothing good that's what. Our liver and kidneys and probably other organs have microscopic holes in them that house these microscopic chemicals. It is here where they stay. Not only there. They eventually get into your blood. Why do you think your blood gets dirty? What do you think it is?

Our American bodies are chemically altered. There is no doubt about this. Did I mention drugs yet? Have I forgot to mention cigarettes? OH I'm sorry, maybe later. I'm not going to say anything about beer. I think beer is food. You know it is.

LIVING DEAD WATER:

Water is not just any water. There is water for the dead then there is water for the living. There is tap water then there is alkalized water. Alkalized water is living water. Alkalized 7.5 to 11.5 is living water. Why? Because it alkalizes you body. Your body is acidic. Everything you eat is acidic.

The only way to get any alkalinity is to eat fruits and green vegetables. Most people don't eat either. Sad but true.

Tap water on the other hand is alkalized through synthetic means. Lye is used to alkalize tap water. But it is used to keep the pipes from rusting. All tap water and bottled water is good enough to drink. But is does not flush out the toxins in the body one hundred percent.

Blood is the life of the body, and water is the life of the blood. Most people have dirty bodies due to the fact that the water they drink cannot flush out the remaining toxins in the body after a good meal. The remaining acidic waste from foods is still present. It is a build up of these toxic wastes that become a problem later on in life.

Sometimes even sooner than expected do we come down with some condition. The toxic waste builds up in our system and our blood becomes sludge thereby causing systems. But people cannot see what is happening inside there bodies. So the water from tap and bottled, while is good for hydration is inefficient for one hundred percent hydration.

So what is happening is that we get some condition that is starting to arise and we go to the doctor and guess what they do? They give us some kind of pill to alleviate the symptoms.

Have you heard of a book called <u>You're Not Sick You're Just Thirsty</u>? This is a very good book. Go find it and read it now.

The bases for all sickness are an acidic state of being.

You are not your body. You are not your thoughts. Your body is a living organism. You have to think like this or you will not understand. You body is in a state of decaying and dying. The water for the dead is the water for the masses, which is tap water and bottled water. Trust me!

City water in many counties and states across this great land of ours is fast becoming non drinkable.

Other liquids for the living dead are sodas. Sodas are highly acidic. Again there is a good reason to drink alkalized water to counter balance the body. Your body right now is in desperate need to have something alkaline going through it. But that is probably not going to happen.

How about all the new caffeine drinks available today? These are highly acidic. In fact everything you buy in the store anywhere is acidic. Why is it this way? Good question.

I don't know, conspiracy maybe.

It is nobody's business to make you healthy except your self. No one is responsible for you except you. No one is going to come along to tell you what is good for you and not good for you. You must figure this out on your own.

Your body is said to be rusting in side because of the non living water it desperately needs. The water available to the masses is causing peoples bodies to massively rust. This is why our society is quickly deteriorating. This essay is the voice of reason. It is a bridge between the two worlds.

The point here is that you not sick. Your body is desperately thirsty. I know this is a radically new concept. But it is not a new concept. The old ways are just that the old ways. We are on the verge of a new society. This is the age on a new dawn. Catch hold of these concepts. This new age is the age of taking care of your own health, learning to stay healthy in other ways other than by the old guard.

Remember nothing is what it seems. Water is not just water. All sodas are different. There are different types of gasoline. There are many types of cars. There are many races of peoples. There are many types of just about everything. Water should hydrate. Think about this new concept. Then look into it and then do something good for your self. I am not in the business of water machines. But I know others who are. This is where I learned it from.

I am a Kangen water student and owner. It takes about thirty days to fully hydrate the body with alkalized water.

This to me says that the body is badly in need of life giving water. Your cells are dry.

In the scriptures Jesus makes a comment about spirits roaming over parched lands looking for a place to call home. What this means is that they occupy people. The reason they have to occupy flesh and blood is because they are hydrants with water. So to become parched is bad for the human body and physic. So there is a plan in place to parch your body so that your life will be cut short. This is the reason for all of the acidic foods and all of the acidic fluids in our society. Is this the conspiracy theory? Of course not, why would we think that.

LIVING DEAD MEDICINE:

The doctors and their medicines; what cannot be said. You have seen the commercials lately, haven't you?

On the one side of the mouth they state what this pill can do then on the other side they state the ten different dead things this pill will cause you. Talk about diabolical. This smacks right into my theory here about the living dead.

Medication is the medicine for the masses. Therefore it is the medication for the living dead. Let me state right up front that we need doctors. We also need medicine. So this makes our situation a paradox.

But the facts are undeniable here that our society is flooded with medicines that our diseases are starting to laugh at them. There is certainly a pill for every ill.

Drugs are a gate way to harder things they say. While on the one hand stay away from hard and illegal drugs but let us give them some of our synthetic drugs in place of it.

Jail them for illicit drugs but let us screw them up with our fake drugs. Talk about twisted here. This is just the way it is currently. Or am I missing something?

I will also state that I do not take any drugs whatsoever. I do not take any prescribed medications. I don't even take aspirin except on rare occasions. I am the better off for it as well.

Do we need medications? Absolutely! But we are on the wrong path. I think everyone should try to wean themselves off any and all medications.

Let me relate a story here. This is a true mother-in-law story. I had this stupid mother-in-law. Boy was she dumb.

She takes pride in being a home school instructor. This woman was once a nurse. OH! She is a real smart one all right. She has had severe depression for a long, long time obviously. She let health deteriorate to the point that she is living in a wheel chair. All of her children take turns taking care of her. Now you say nothing unusual about this. I say hog wash, watch this. She takes 46 medications a day.

Again you think that this is not out of the norm. I again say let's do the math.

Popping 46 pills a day times seven days comes to 322 pills per week. Now let's take this one step further. 322 pills per week times 52 weeks comes to a whopping 16,744 pills per year. Are you starting to see the picture here. Now let's put the nail in the coffin here. 16,744 times the last ten years comes to 167,440. This is the amount of pills this woman has taken over the last ten years. Not to mention the cost of it all. My hearing has heard that this woman last year in the year of 2010 spent over $10,000 in medications with insurance. Talk about astoundingly stupid. Now get this. I introduced her to Kangen water. She vehemently did not want this life giving water. This is not only just stupid but is fucking insane. Do you get my drift here?

Now you say, "well pity for her." You should lay off of her. I say she is getting exactly what she deserved. Death!

She is living in the land of the dead. She takes the pills of the dead. The pills actually stop her from dying. This is the amazing part. Am I judging her to harshly? Well yes. Do I have a right to this? Again I say hell yes! Here is the reason why. I have had severe pain in my body after thirty years of welding. I went on a campaign to rid my self of my symptoms. I used other methods that did the job well. I can sit here and see the two worlds with open eyes. Now I think she has no place trying to teach my children anything, period. I am living in health and will for a long time to come. She has taken over 167,440 pills over the last ten years and has spent over $100,000 or more on medications and health care practices. My cost has not exceeded over two thousand dollars. I think we have a mental pity party going on here in her head. Am I now a loving son in-law?

Now I will say to you who are you going to listen too? Will I ever need a doctor? Probably so, but not any time soon, God willing. I'm sure she is not the only person out there who looks to the medical establishment for pity. These people have inside mental conditions that look to the doctors to not only treat a phantom symptom but to gain pity as well.

Let re tell you another story here. This is a good husband story about his dear little wife. I married this young woman sometime back who had inside mental issues.

Of course being not a doctor of mental health I was not up to date on mental health. Well she had issues alright. When I first met her we thought she might have become pregnant. I said great sister. Very nice. I'm down for this. She said early on OH! My pain! I need a hospital. Well, I rushed her to the hospital. The doctors said let us look at your problem. I waited in the waiting room. This was a tubal pregnancy she says. They say ok lets have a look. They operate and low and behold there was nothing there. The doctors were baffled. They found nothing that could substantiate her claims. Well, this was the beginning of my education about mental illness and medications. During the years that followed more bad situations occurred. I mean serious issues came about in my life as long as I was associated with her. Over a long period of time I noticed a bad habit of hers. She was always going to the doctors and claiming to have some condition. Now you never know right. So the thinking goes. After about seven years the doctors were turning her down. It was not long after that her world turned upside down. In all actuality it was trying to turn right side up. By trying to turn her life right side up she committed suicide. The outside authorities were shutting her down thereby trying to make things right. She could not stand this and ended her life because there was nobody to feel pity for her any longer. This is a true story. Sad as though it is.

So now you know where it is that I am coming from. Can anyone understand my story here? I have my views solidified in chaos. I was born into upside down thinking that has righted itself. So this is why I am the way I am.

LIVING DEAD RELATIONSHIPS:

Do you remember the stories above? There is more to come. How about this one? My second wife. Talk about a twisted relationship.

Here is a story about more upside down thinking. Shall we say upside down and backward inter changeably. I cannot speak for all relationships so I do know about mine from the inside. I also know about others from the outside looking in.

Again with Le feminine. I found somebody else, yea!

We had two children. Things seemed almost alright in the beginning. But I saw the twisted signs up front. But ignored them for now. But over a period of time they kept getting stronger and stronger. Bottom line is this she used me to get the seed. Then over a period of time did away with me. She phased me out like I was an employee. My job has been done away with.

Is this abnormal? Not even close. I see it all the time in relationships. It is all over the place. All kinds of women are doing exactly the same thing. Although covertly. Is it justified? Probably so in many cases. But I truly believe it was completely unnecessary in my case. I did all the right things that were expected of me in my position. I saw the end coming years before it ever came to pass and did everything in my power to avoid it. But in the end it was destined because of the simple fact that it takes two people in agreement. But she did hit me with all sorts of irrationality along the way.

This became my psychological training ground. It was this time period over a 14 year stretch that my views of things and the way the people were around me were put into sharp focus. I had my male view I sure did. But I allowed principle to take hold primarily. In other words I held my tongue until the right time. This woman put every thing into a negative spin. This was the same path my first wife had. I knew the end result. So I am in a position where I must defend my self and my future.

Now meanwhile I was learning to make beautiful pieces of art. So my mind set was right. I over came serious health issues. Again my mind set was in the right spot. In other words I am right on Johnny.

But she made me out to be Johnny trouble. She did not know it at the time but I did have a Mexican p it bull homey from South Phoenix days that was a very bad Johnny. I mean for real. So I was not a bad Johnny. But she used her twisted power to covert this family man into a bad Johnny. To this day she pretends to be afraid. But it is all pretend. She has introduced phantoms from the mind. I will not step into those pretend shoes. All of this to say that she has opened the door for a bad Johnny to come in and really be bad. What I am trying to say is this she is getting worse with time in her mental state. She cannot see this. But her world is turning upside down. This is other wise known as a toxic relationship. But her destiny is opposite mine. My destiny is to be s story teller of truth and honesty. Hers is to be its opposite. "You will know them by their fruits."

What will her future look like? Well, Lets see here. She cannot have a great relationship because she had one and destroyed it completely. So this is her history. She does not know how to build creatively. She will continue to have health issues because she will not change for the better. She will continue to have the same point of view and stay unhappy because she cannot change. Her health mind and body will worsen because she is on her mother's pill popping feel sorry for my self vain. She will massively struggle and possibly commit suicide later on down the road like my last wife did. Any woman who replaces her man with a shit eating dog that eats everything in the house and all the things their in is in bad shape. Any woman that Throws a family man out the door that does her laundry and dirty dishes is completely unhealthy, and puts dazzling metal sculptures on her walls is sick. Any woman who cannot appreciate a man that gets out of the house and reinforces a shovel to deal with her properties issues has a misguided mind set. Honestly what ever happened to the marriage vows? This came down to a power issue. She had to show me that she could exercise her power over me. This is a mind set that is irrational. This is her mind disease. But this is the mind disease of many in our society. I see it all over the place. It is a total lack of honesty. They are mind generated false truths. This is other wise known as her sin.

She could not comprehend that I was an integrated thinker. Such are people everywhere. How could I explain that I see your mind disease? Do you get my drift here? So goes the living dead relationships. The divorce rate in this country is well over the 50% mark and climbing. Nothing we can do about this.

The human physic is under going an invasion of insanity. There is a reason for this. It is said that a crack in the watchtower door way has been opened and a few demons are now running loose in our subconscious. More on this later.

What this story has revealed is that all good things are being perverted. Our sanity is being challenged. All things are headed south. If you think what I am saying is perverted then just wait in time and all things will get even worse. If you think me a bad Johnny then wait a spell you will see the real bad Johnny immerge and it will not be me.

Live now is my advice. Get rid of that asshole you're with that is making your life miserable.

As I go about my daily business life I encounter all kinds of internal subtleties that chaos is just below the surface. Can you feel it?

All I can say is internalize these truths. Prepare your self for what is about to come. Pray often. Find others like your self for sanities sake. Amen.

We are living in times where we are having massive fear, massive doubt, and massive mistrust everywhere. These truths are right in front of you all you have to do is stop are look at them.

LIVING DEAD BELIEF:

I think the previous stories tell of misguided thinking. Misguided thinking is not new, but is more prevalent these last days than lets say 20 years ago. We are headed towards the last hour. The belief system is what we will examine here. The criminal mind set: The criminal mind set is the thinking of the criminal. That is to take values without rightfully compensating. It is an unequal value exchange.

Usurp means: to seize and hold by force or without right.

Here is another true story. Since my writing these essays I hired a young woman to design a web site. I hand selected her because she had the talent I desired. We agreed on everything we discussed. I paid her $500.00 cash and we sealed the deal with a hand shake. I thought everything was cool. Now she did not deliver. In fact this is the third time she has failed me. This third time she now wants to negotiate a contract. She has asked for more money and commitment. Mean while she has kept the money I gave her. She has yet to deliver. I have been waiting for 21 days now.

Do you see any thing wrong here? Or are you a person who can not see anything wrong. If you are the latter then you are problematic yourself. First off this is the third time. Next since she has my money and materials she is using them as hostage. Third is the delay. She has not held up her end of the bargain. This is the criminal mind set I am talking about.

How about the three other stories I related to you previously? The criminal mind set was there as well. It is done covertly. These people don't think I can see it but that is not the case. Truth is every one employs it. This is why there is so much domestic violence. These types of manipulations are a constant in relationships. Everybody is jockeying for position here. Instead of being honest about things people usurp values, the other party sees injustice and gets angry. That is when retaliation happens.

We are a people who cannot get it honest anymore. I have even witnessed a Jehovah's Witness lie and accuse me falsely. The technique is simple. It involves the use of non-sequiturs. It is the misuse of words by twisting the facts using non sequiturs. It is taking the facts and perverting them to make them upside down.

How about another true story: Here goes. I had this dear old friend who was and still a Jehovah's Witness. We were pretty good friends. After all they are good people.

We know that to be self evident. I took a job out of town and was not around that much. But during my time in the kingdom hall I had touched a woman on the arm in honest gesture. Well I must have done it to another sometime because the complaint was that I had touched a sister.

These three elders called me to the back room to give me the third degree, nicely of course. Now bear in mind that I have not been in this kingdom hall for months because I have been working out of town. So the alleged touch happened four to six months past history.

So they made known to me that I had done a bad thing.

I had touched a sister. She is said to have been troubled by this light touch on the arm. I did not submit to these brothers. I let them know that they were dealing with some mind disease and that this cannot be a bad thing. They made it sound like I was a bad Johnny. I took authority over this meeting. My anger did rise. I knew that I was dealing with the mind virus right away. I made this known to them and they did not understand what I was trying to tell them. They went right on with there chiding. Seeing that they dismissed me my temper rose another notch. I asked them what the word of God had to say about this subject and they did not know the answer. I reminded them that the word of God says that we are to greet one another with a holy kiss. Meaning that we are to be loving through touch, hugs, hand shakes in a reverent way. They agreed with the statement. But continued to chide me and making me into the bad Johnny. My temper went up one more notch. I thought to my self this is the same thing that my wives had done. This can't be happening to me in this here Jehovah's Witness kingdom hall.

I left and went home far away and was deeply disturbed about this. My old friend came to see me and we discussed this subject. He made some startling statements that led me to conclude he had set me up. He was angry that I was not going to become one of them. He was jealous that he had spent so much time that I was like an investment. So he used this situation to make me submit or get out. A kind of like a do or die thing. Do you think he is man enough to admit this? I don't think so. But this brother displayed the criminal mind set. I called there shit on it and they became defeated foes. But get this, they can't see it. Upon departure of the kingdom hall I stated that this accusatory dragon that you are displaying I have slain that dragon. Again they had no clue as to my meaning. I will tell you though. This dragon I have been slaying is through the acts of others for the last 20 years in all my relationships. They were talking to a true Chourist warrior and did not know or recognize it. How sad. I am a man that has been fighting the good fight of faith all of my life and they did not know it. This is the belief of the living dead.

How about one more story: In 2003 I created a word board game that was based on the scriptures. Just like anyone I wanted to take it up a notch. So I went on the hunt for a graphic artist. I found one that had his own print shop.

I thought cool this man knows business. I can trust him. I met him at his home and we agreed upon everything. I handed him my project and he said he showed enthusiasm.

I paid him in cash and walked away. He never did do the work. He gave me excuses that lasted four months. I tried to believe in him. But truth be told he just didn't do the work and never had plans to do it either. Through the years I encountered him around town. I asked other business about him and they said you have to watch you ass around him He will take your money and will not perform. I don't think he is doing business in that town anymore. He has made sure he screwed everyone in town before he left. To this day he had my material. He never had the nerve to bring it back. Never mind though I recreated it and made it better. I still have it to this day. Again this is the belief of the living dead.

LIVING DEAD RELIGION:

Living dead religion says it all. Hey! I go to church. I have always gone to church. I grew up in a Seventh Day Adventist church. This is my early child hood history. I spent six years in a charismatic church in Texas in the early 1980's. I have spent large amounts of time in a large Baptist setting in North Phoenix, AZ. I have spent the last several years going to three services on Sunday two of which being full gospel and the third service is with Jehovah's Witness.

So, do I speak with the voice of authority? Absolutely not! But I do speak with my own mind set I will state this odd concept here. I see some things as a constant reoccurring night mare. I have my faith you know.

But in recent years I keep experiencing this reoccurring night mare in the day time. It always happens on Sunday while in church. It has always been a constant nagging for over thirty years. I finally identified it. You are not going to like what it is. I shall call it God of the living dead. See! I told you will not like it. It's the old adage that God is dead.

Well, they were right. God is dead in the fact that God will not allow you as a human to live in peace. Sex is bad. Drugs are bad. Looking at your fine neighbors ass is just plain corrupt. This brings bad vibrations to the human race.

It is death to my organism. Therefore God is the God of the living dead. Get it? God is not for your organism. He is against it in every area. So God has to be eliminated from the equation. This is the message of the lord of eternal light will say. All of the little pathetic lambs will have to go with it. They are all useless.

Why do you call it that? Well hell you don't know child? Ok stupid let daddy explain this thing to you. You are such stupid little lambs.

As I sat in church on many occasions I would hear that we were in a war out in the world. Then I would go to work on Monday and war with my inner self. I would hear that we are in the last days and we must prepare our selves for the coming Lord of Lords. I hear that we are the little lambs of God and that we are to be prosecuted. I hear lots of stories about the Biblical past that have no problem solving capabilities in the present tense, always looking to the past to solve present tense life. I have had deep inner turmoil since child hood. I need something that is good for my organism now in the present tense. I never did find it in church. I had to look else ware in life. So I went looking for my salvation. I did not need eternal salvation for I already had this, which of course was a disputable concept with the Jehovah's Witness. They think you must earn it everyday.

Wrong! Wrong! , Wrong! I have heard a life time of teachings. All are contrary to one another. Which is the true way I'm confused? All claim to be the true way, baffling.

So what is the point here? Well I have figured out that the path of the Christian concept is a false vein. First, I have to deny my organism as a man. Second I have to give up all things that are impure in a world that is un-pure. Third is my strict belief system that all things are bad in a world that believes the exact opposite. But there is more.

No matter what it is that I believe in the Christian belief vein I end up in the wrong end of town. I end up in the wrong situation. I end up in the wrong relationship. My Christian beliefs have no earthly value. I finally figured out the real secret to the power on this earth. It is called energy and vibration. This is the key to the scripture. This is the language behind the scriptures. Once you understand this concept all things become crystal clear.

So, do I believe still in the Lord? The answer is absolutely! But not like you think. I am like all of you, I have a duel mind set. This is my unique position. This essay will resonate with all who read it because I am nothing but a conduit between these two worlds. My mission is to prepare you for what is to come upon this old world. So in order to accomplish this mission I must first tear down your current belief system through the power of reduction. You God damn little lamb! Your God has set you up for the slaughter. Both God and god are about to harvest your dumb ass.

You see you and I are really not shit. We actually don't know diddly squat. It is from this mind set that the watching gods judge us all. It is not a matter of beliefs per se. It is a matter of what energy pattern you are being held in. It is about being free or being in bondage. All of the world is in bondage and can't see it. They are too used to it. But the world is the world is the world. I know the world just as you do. Except I know it from my inner troubled view. My life's quest has always been about answers to my inner turmoil.

All religion is said to be is a teacher of good moral character. But what value it brings in this earths realm is another question. Is it wrong? No! By all means continue.

My mission is to bring to you the dominating thought pattern behind the world physic. It is diabolic you know. My mission statement is to cut through all the bull shit and bring to you cutting edge thinking for the coming of Horus. We are in the new dawn of the age of Aeon of Horus. Aeon means: indefinitely a long time. Horus is another name of Choronzon. Choronzon is the true name of Satan in heaven.

If you ask me where on earth did I get that? I will tell you never you mind where I got that. Just be grateful that I found it and brought it to you. We are in a new dawn of time. We are in the age of the stargate. We are in the time of great wonders due to technology. We are in the greatest time of the history of man kind. We are going to see some of the most awesome things unfold. So sit back and enjoy the show. Remove your self from all commitments and desire mobility above all things.

Religion will under go a surgery. This essay is just a warning of sorts. If you are a Christian then your new mission is to see things in the new light. I shall call this concept the light of dark. Darkness will come to light.

Darkness will show its head. The prince of darkness will pay us a little visit. He wants to dwell with man. He wants to come out of the cosmos and come to earth and play god. We as god damn humans will god damn worship him too, since he has come from so far away. We will welcome him with open arms god damn it. Join him in his quest of purging the earth of the mystic mind set.

This will be his mission. His mission is to rid the earth of the God believing humans. His mission has the blessings of God all over them. He has the perfect right to chop your head of if you worship the true God. He will do away with the world's governments. He will set us free of tyranny. He will become our true god on this earth, so all the earth will worship him. Are you ready? Well stupid, get ready. He is here already. He has been invoked. The crack in the watchtower has been slightly ajar and a few demons have come in and have occupied the earth's subconscious. You know this to true.

This is just a snapshot of what is to come. As a welder and fabricator I have my own solid view of what hell is. All of my life I have been subject to fire and ice, if not the one then the other. This has been my training ground. So my position is that I don't have to be lovely in introducing these things to you. You will learn from me through fire and ice. God damn it!

If your religion has made you into a lost little lamb then you are prepared for the slaughter. If you are a believer of old then off with your head. Your religion will be blamed for all the earth's deceptions. You and your belief in God is responsible for the worlds wars. Your God is guilty of the earth's deception. He is mystical! Where is this true God? He is no where to save you now Christian, because your God is unreal. We live in a world full of half truths because of your God. Your God has caused our world to become under darkness. We all are in bondage because of this unreal God. We have got to do away with this concept of sin. We are not free as long as we are accused of being in sin. Screw this God belief. Your God beliefs are the reason we have the mind disease and have to be purged from this earth. This means you Christian. Our stated goal is off with your head. We no longer will put up with this guilt from the mystical God. We want to live in our world guilt free.

Can you feel me dog? Can you feel my vibrations here?

You want to serve the true God? Then we will eliminate you.

We don't want you here on our earth. We claim this earth to be God free. Our god is of this world! He will save us from the true God. Our god loves us and wants to spend eternity with us. He is the god of pleasure. He is the god of the flesh and we are flesh and blood. We will serve the sun god on Sunday. So if you go to church on Sunday we can live with that. Whatever you do don't serve the true God on the true Sabbath which is Saturday. For this is this Fourth commandment. This is in violation of our dark gods principles. This is why our dark disciples changed the Sabbath day from Saturday to Sunday.

This ladies and gentleman is the doctrine of the beast. How do you like it? Is it upside down and twisted? This is the new reality. Welcome to the age of Horus. Just remember Choronzon loves you and wants to slaughter you so that he will have company throughout eternity.

Hey! SATAN is not a bad fellow. Just because he has a hatred for you doesn't make him all bad. Hey! Your God has and will slaughter as many people as he does. So who is bad here?

It is believed among the Jehovah's Witness that Satan and his comrades were kicked out of heaven in 1914. In occult circles the age of Horus was ushered in at around the same time, they state in 1904. This would explain for the earth's demise since that time period. True or not this is the beliefs. Now the watch tower is a kingdom hall study pamphlet. They have adopted this concept. The watch tower in the occult is the watch tower of the earth in the spirit realm. They are located in all four corners of the earth. These are strong holds that keep the evil spirits at bay. They are they watch towers of the earth. These watch towers have gate keepers and have gate keys. Nothing passes these gate keepers unless Jehovah allows it. The keys of this realm have been given to man. Man is now in possession of the gate keys. Man has cracked the gate open. Nothing in this earth's realm is allowed in except through mankind.

Man kind will initiate the Apocalypses. Satan cannot come into this realm unless asked in. In this country and through the earth these dark secret orders have invoked Choronzon, conjured him up so to speak. They have called for him to return. The lord of darkness has heard and will enter if not already. But the earth has been preparing for him. The stage has been set for his glorious return, and what a show he will bring. Long live the lord of darkness. Long live the light bearer.

It is believed that Enochian evocations has cracked open the doors to the watch towers enough to let in a foul wind to blow through the common subconscious mind of the human race at or around the time of 1904 to 1914, roughly.

Spirits are mental, not material. They dwell in the depths of the mind and communicate with us through our dreams, unconscious impulses, and more rarely in waking visions. They affect our feelings and our thoughts beneath the level of our conscious awareness. Sometimes they are able to control our actions, either partially as in the case of irrational and obsessive behavior patterns, or completely as in the case of full possession.

Through us, by using us as their physical instruments, and through us, are they able to influence physical things. The Enochian Angels that brought mankind the gate keys over four centuries ago teach us that not only must humanity itself initiate the cosmic drama of the Apocalypse through the magic formula delivered to mankind. But the stupid humans must also be the physical actors that bring about the plagues, wars and famines described with such chilling eloquence in the book of Revelation. We have cracked the gate and let the demons of Choronzon into our minds by certain ritual working. They have not found a welcome place in our minds all at once: But they have wormed their way into our subconscious and they make their homes there slowly over a period of time.

Once they have taken a foothold we as humans will find ourselves powerless to prevent them from turning our thoughts and actions toward chaotic and destructive ends. These Apocalyptic spirits will set person against person nation against nation, gradually increasing the degree of madness, and chaos, among stupid humans until at last the horror of Revelation has been realized upon the world stage. The corruption of human thoughts and feelings may take several generations to bring to fruition. We have seen this first hand since the beginning of the 20th century.

Since the beginning of the 20th century we have seen two world wars, and the Nazi horrors and death camps.

This also explains the world's religions in decline and soulless science taking its place. This also explains the moral and ethical bankruptcy of modern times and the increase in senseless crimes of violence.

We don't have to wait to long before the gates of the watch tower will swing wide open and the horrors on earth will be in full swing. If this chilling mythic scenario ever comes to pass, the wars of the 20th century will seem bucolic to those who survive the slaughter.

How will Choronzon enter from the cosmic realm? Good question. Personally, If I tell you now promise me you will not repeat this. Let me whisper this in your ear so as no one can hear this. Shhhh! I think he will come through the Star gate. Why else is the United States occupying the land of Nimrod?

THIRTEEN REASONS WHY YOU'RE SICK, BROKE & DUMB

MORTGAGE-HOME-BUYING

There it is a perception that real estate is the place to make money. While this is true in one aspect it a misconception on the other. When it comes to your home (house) separate from the land there is some things to consider.

LAND

Land cannot devalue. The concept is that land cannot be taken from its current location. Land cannot be hidden from view. So we are not talking land here or its value. The point of this memo is the financing of your house, dwelling place, or the structure where you lay your body down at night.

Does your home have value? Sure it does. But not like you think. Think of it this way, you know that when you buy a new car it immediately loses its value by several thousands of dollars just as soon as you drive it off the lot. If you bought a car for $25,000 then drove it straight to another dealer for a trade chances are 111% he will lower it by at least 3,000. This represents a 12% automatic reduction right off the top.

Your home is no different. Your home will devalue over time. It's understandable that you think of your home as an investment. This is true but not 100% true. Your home and land can be considered your bank account, but only if you take really good care of it. In fact it is nearly impossible to keep it in brand new condition thereby holding its value.

From an appraisers stand point, your banks stand point and from an investors stand point, your home loses its value the minute you buy it.

DEPRECIATION

Straight line depreciation. This means a 2% reduction each year it stands. If your home was built 50 years ago it should have A 100% depreciation. But you know this is not exactly true. But this is just an analysis to start with. What this is saying is that real estate and the world of financing is very, very fluid. The mind of a developer is not the mind of an investor. They are similar but not the same. A banker also thinks differently than an appraiser. But they all have one thing in common and that is to make a profit.

So, I ask this question again, can you make a profit on your home? The answer has to be a sound no! Your home depreciates while your land appreciates. This is why your lender does not want an appraisal on your home before you buy. He doesn't want to know what it is worth exactly.

The higher he thinks its worth the more interest will be paid over the life of the loan. The lenders point of view is to get you into the home via his financing and lock you into an interest rate that will put all your money in his pocket for the next 30 years.

Your lack of knowledge hurts you in the long run. When I say "hurt" I mean in the purse. In other words your stupidity or not knowing screws you for the life of the loan.

Let's run the numbers: A House can cost easily 300,000. A 300,000 loan @ let's say a 6%. You will pay 18,000 hard earned dollars just in interest per year. That equals to 1,500 per month. 300,000 @ 6% over a 30 year time span comes to A whopping 540,000. 540,000- 300,000= 240,000 difference. 300,000 Divided by 540,000= A 55.55% above the loan amount. So we have a 155% pay back.

Let's look at a 200,000 loan. A 200,000 loan amount with A 7% interest. This is 14,000 per year in payments @ 1,166.66 monthly. 200,000 @ 7% for 30 years comes to 420,000. That is a 47.61 percent above the loan amount. In other words A 148% payback.

Now, I must say from my point of view this is not a good picture. Who is zooming who? But you say "well, I'll get it all back concept of time value of money? Well, it plays a part of devaluation. We will explore this and another concept later. This appears to be a win lose deal.

MANUFACTURED HOUSING

Manufactured homes are A great way to live. I know I have spent more than a decade living in a manufactured home. I sure do love them dearly. I loved mine so much I spent many a time in my shop creating metal sculptors to hang on my wall and to this day that is where they still are. But let's run some numbers here.

My 2000 model was $100,000. It has 2,533 square feet. To place it on this piece of land An additional $65,000 was needed. Now, I must add that the contractors who did all the work done an outstanding job in the month of February. They were truly ducks. But the cost of things is what is in question. $165000 x .06 interest = $9900 per year in interest. $9900 x30 years = $297,000. $297,000 Plus $165,000= $462,000. This is a 136% payback return to the bank. Having said that, let's move into the city.

MOBILE HOMES AND LOTS

Now I know that things cost a lot of money just to move a mobile home. I think mobile homes on rented lots is and should be a crime or at least against the law punishable by heavy fines including jail. No! I don't mean the ownership silly, I mean the home owner not being able to own the land underneath it. To me I see it as entrapment. This is the crime. The home owner has no security. Land ownership is security. You are being robbed, looted, railroaded.

Let's say you have a lot rent per month of 300 to 500. This is reasonable assumption. Let's analyze the 300 first. You pay 300x12=3600 per year. That comes to a $108,000 over a 30 year period and you own nothing. You still have no solid security. Now if your house cost $100,000 @ 6% that would be another $120,000. 120,000+108.000= $228,000. $228,000 divided 360 months is $633.33 per month.

It is not the payment per month that bothers me it is the final number stretched for so long. On top of it you could be out of a home any day because you own not the land. Personally, I would rather own the land without the house than have a house without the land.

Now Let's take a look at the $500 number. $500 per month x12=$6,000 per year. $6,000x30 years=$180,000. Let's use the above number for the house and add another $120,000. $120,000+180,000=$300,000. $300,000 divided by 360 payments =833.33 per month. Again you own nothing. "Well, I own my house, you say you. Well, says I "You can be asked to move your damn house lady. Because I sold the land underneath you while you were sleeping. You have six months to a year to get your house of this property or we bulldoze it". Now ,what have you got? Absolutely nothing. All your hard work, all your money, all your sweat, and all your love gone to shit because you were not smart enough to put your house on your own land. Don't think it can't happen to you? Think again.

Remember, an investors view is unlike your own. This is not a win-win deal. It is not exactly a win lose either. But things are changing in the real estate market. So, look out!

RENT

Got to love those renters, better yet, got to have compassion for those renters. From an ownership standpoint, I do feel a deep sense of compassion for them all. Are they any worse than the rest of us? The answer is both yes and no. In the final analysis they are probably better off just renting. I will explain later If I can remember to. Let's run the numbers-$500 per month X 12 = $6,000 per year. $6,000 year x15 years = $90,000. $6,000 year X 30years = $180,000. $600 mo X 12= $7200 year. $7,200 year X 15 = $108,000. $7200 year X 30 year = $216,000. $700 per mo X 12 = $8,400 year. $8,400 year X 15 = $126,000. $8,400 year X 30 year = $252,000. $800 per mo X 12 = $9,600 year. $9,600 X 15 = $144,000. $9,600 year X 30 year = $288,000. $900 per mo = $10,800 year. $10,800 year X 15 = $162,000. $10,800 X 30 year = $324,000. $1,000 mo X 12 = $12,000 year. $12,000 year X 15 year = $180,000. $12,000 year X 30 year = $360,000. Should I go on, or do you get the picture?

This is where your money is going. In the end you own nothing.

Now from an investors point of view. Let's say he bought your building for $500,000. A 24 unit. $1,000 X 24 = $24,000 month. $24,000 mo X 12 = $288,000 year. $288,000 year X 15 year = $4,320,000. $288,000 X 30 year = $8,640,000. Now there are operating expenses of all kinds and managers salary etc, etc. Again I say who is zooming who? Is this a win lose deal or what. It is and it isn't.

EXPENSES

When it comes to home or land ownership; rent, mortgage, utilities are not the only expenses. There are multiple expenditures both inside and outside the home. Inside the home there is everything that makes a house a home. Outside there is all those things concerning maintenance, which includes garden, sheds, tools, etc, etc.

If you own livestock then there is feed, hay, equipment fencing, and barns. Let's not forget the mower or the tractor. Each and every one of these items cost more than you have in your piggybank. Why not include your time. Time is money, you know. This is why you don't have any money to spare, which is why your flat broke.

How do you get around it, you ask? Rent an apartment that's what you do. With renting you have no outside responsibilities. You also gain your precious time back. So by taking this route you are free X two (doubly free).

J.O.B.

What foul word haven't you said about your job? Right, that's what I thought. You've said them all. Well, I'm in total agreement, screw your job. Better yet screw your boss, take him for a ride. Take the company for a ride. If you think your company is going to stay true to you, think again. Better yet, just turn on the television, talk to your neighbor, and they will all have a horror story about their place of employment.

I liken it to swimming up stream, Everyday battling the current. All jobs are stressful and taxing on your body and mind daily. It is a daily bombardment of toxins that destroy body, mind, and soul. These toxins destroy your immune system. Then they will shit can you. Better yet you will be shit canned eventually anyway. If you do not under stand what I'm saying here then you are either in denial of not aware. Whenever you come into contact with the fabricated world there will be automatic stress. What I mean is that which is unnatural or manmade.

The reason you have a job is because you perceive you need one. Your society, schooling, education system has conditioned you to think that way. Your family all had jobs. You were destined for a job. I am no better. Once you have a job you will become trapped, because your bills don't stop and you need to pay them. So you spend all you time at a job to accomplish this .It becomes a never ending cycle, day in day out. Chances are while you're at your job, you will encounter some big assholes, a bitch or two, a couple of shit asses a prick, several bitches, snitches, loudmouths, a dick head, and at least one dumb ass. If you're lucky you might encounter a nymph.

In my view I'd rather spend my time with a hooker than a jealous bootlicker. And guess what, that's not all. You get to encounter various people who you give opportunity to stab you in the back. Then there is the no chance for advancement. Talk about dead end. Oh!, I forgot to mention you can spend 8 10 12 hours each and everyday with them. 5 to 7 days a week. That comes to 40 to 60 hours a week. 160 to 240 hours a month. That's 2000 to 3000 hours a year. But here is the best part, they really never become your true friends. They never really care about you. They only pretend to.

You're thinking my job can't do without me. Well, if they think you believe that then it is time for you to go. Once you think you have it made BAM! They slap you down and kick your ass down the highway. It will all come down quick, cold, and calculated. This will leave you lost, bewildered, confused.

What the hell just happened? Where did all that negative come from? I didn't deserve that. Nothing makes sense.

Tell me my friend, does any of this sound familiar? Sure, it has to, question is how many times. My point is this, there is absolutely no security on job. Today's managers make everything impossible. So learn to think for your self. Be more independent of this system of things. I know a lot of people who do a lot of different things. The more I watch them the more I realize that they are all dying inside daily because of their job.

Jobs are not life giving they are life sucking. Right now as you are thinking about your job tell me how do you feel?

Managerial policies are designed to screw your vibration by weighing you down with all things negative. It is loaded with double speak, double talk. They purposely lay all the work, responsibilities, and blame onto the low cast slaves. This leaves them with nothing to do but shuffle paper work and when they are done with that they sit around and think of ways they can put more blame, responsibility, and guilt on you. This is modern day slavery.

But this is all by intelligent design. The technique is called back door control, side door intimidation. There view of you is less than human. Tell me my friend, how do you feel about all of this? Well, then I rest my case. Now let's run some numbers and see if all of this shit you put up with is really worth it.

If you had a $10.00 hour job and worked 40 hour week. $10.00 x 40 =$400.00 per week x .33 for taxes, 400 x .33 = 132.00. $400 - 132 = $268.00 take home. $268.00 x 52 weeks = $13,936 per years spendable income. $13936 x 30 years = 418,080 spendable income more or less.

First of all, by today's living standards this is below poverty. If you pay $500.00 per month for rent this comes to 46.64% of income. 500 divided by 1,072 = 46.64. If you pay $600 in rent then 55.97%. 600 divided by 1,072 = 56% rounded. If you had an $11.00 hour job, that comes to $440.00 per week. $440 x .33 = $145.20 in taxes. $440-145.20 = $294.80 x 52 weeks = $15,329.60 per year. $15,329.60 x 30 years = $459,888 spendable income. $600 rent x 12 month = 7,200 per year. 7,200 per year x 30 year = $216,000 paid over this time period. This comes to 46.96%. 216,000 divided by 459,888 = 47% rounded. How about $700 per month rent at $11.00 hour? $700 x 12 month = $8,400 per year. $8,400 x 30 years = $252,000 paid over this time period. This comes to 54% of income on rent. $252,000 divided by $459,000 = 54.36%. $700 mo rent at 12.00 hour. $700 x 12 mo =8,400. $8,400 x 30 years = $252000 paid rent over this time period. This comes to 50%. $252,000 divided by $501,696 = 50.22%. How about $800 per month at $11.00 hour $800 x 12 mo = $9,600 year. $9,600 year x 30 year = $288,000 rent paid over this time period. This comes to 63% rounded. $288,000 divided by $459,888 = 62.74%. Now let's try $12.00 hour. $12.00 hour x40 hours = $480 week. $480 x .33 = $158.40 in taxes. $480 -$158.40 = $321.60 week. This comes to $16,723.20 per year spendable income. $16,723.60 x 30 year = $501,696. Let's start rent at $700 month. This comes to $8,400 per year. Over a 30 year period this comes to $252,000. This comes to 50%. $252000 divided by $501,696 = 50.22%. Now at $800 month, $800 x 12 = 9,600. $9600 x 30 year = $288,000. This comes to 57% of income. $288,000 divided by $501,696 = 57.40%. Now we go to $13.00 hour job. $13.00 x 40 hour week = $520.week $520 x .33 = $171.60 in taxes. $520 - $171.60 = $348.40 take home. $348 x 52 weeks = $18,116.80 per year spend able income. $18,160.80 year x 30 year = $543,504. So you make $13.00 hour and pay $700 mo rent. This comes to $8,400 per year. $8,400 per year x 30 year = $252,000. This comes to 46%. $252,000 divided by $543,504 = 46.36%. Now at $800 mo rent x 12 = $9,600 year. $9,600 year x30 year = $288,000. This comes to 53% rounded. $288,000 divided by $543,504 = 52.98%. $900 month rent at $13.00 hour. $900 x 12 = $10,800 year. $10,800 year x 30 years = $324,000. This comes to 60% rounded. $324,000 divided by $543,504= 59.61%. If you worked a $14.00 hour job at 40 hours week, that would $560. $560.00 x .33 = $184.80. $540 -184.50 = $355.50 take home. $355.00 = 52 weeks = $18,486 per year. $18,486 x

30 years = $554,580. $700 rent x12 month = $8,400. $8,400 x 30 years = $252,000 rent paid over this period of time. This comes to 45% of income spent on rent. $252000 divided by $554,580 = 45.43. $800.00 month rent would come to $800 x 12 month = 9,600 year. $9,600 year x 30 years = $288,000 in rent receipts, which comes to 52% rounded. $288,000 divided by $554,580 = 51.93%. $800 per month x 12 month = $9,600. $9,600 per year x 30 years =$288,000, which comes to 52% rounded. $288,000 divided by $554,580 = 51.93%. $900 per month x 12 months = $10,800 year. $10,800 per year x 30 years = $324,000. This comes to 58% rounded. $288,000 divided by $554,580 = 58.42%. Now let's try working for $15.00 hour. $15.00 hour x 40 hour week = $600.00 week $600.00 x .33 = $198.00. 600 - 198 = $402.00 take home. $402 x 52 weeks = $20,904 per year income. $20,904 x 30 years = $627120. If your rent was $800 per month that would be $9,600 year X 30 years = $288,000. This would come to 46% rounded in come going to rent. $288,000 divided by $627,120 = 45.92%. $900 per month x 12 month = $10,800 per year. $10,800 x 30 year = $324,000. This comes to 52% rounded. $324,000 divided by $627,120 = 51.66%. So now that we are making more let's find a place for $1,000 per month. $1,000 x12 month = $12,000 per year in rent. $12.000 per year x 30 years = $360,000. This comes to 57% rounded. $360,000 divided by $627,120 = 57.40%.

Also, we must not forget that during this time you would have worked in one year's time a total of 2,080 hours. 40 hours week x 52 weeks = 2,080. 52 weeks a year x 30 years = 62,400 hours. In the end what is that you own? That's right absolutely nothing. That's why this report was written. Most people do not stop to realize what price they are paying. Nor do they stop to count the cost. Welcome to reality. It doesn't make sense once you step back and take a look at it, does it?

LET'S RECAP

The rent you pay with either home owner ship or renting you are truly losing most or all of your money. I like to refer a mortgage as rent mortgage. There are differences don't get me wrong, like freehold estate, which is owner ship interest. But these are our choices and the choices I wish were better. At these wages and mortgage rents the payer is dishing out form 45% to 58%. This is unacceptable. A lender looks at your finances and judges by what he sees and determines whether or not if you qualify for a loan.

One criterion is your income to debt ratio, also a 2.5. Meaning the sales price has to be no more than two and a half times your income. With real estate being so high and wages so low apartments have a greater occupancy rate. Like I said before, "renting may be the smarter way to go in the long run." I do not say this lightly. I can confidently say it because I have lived my last 15 years on large acreage and it has been extremely tough. Mostly Pioneer style hard labor. More about this later.

TAXES

Lessen the amount of taxes you owe. You can do this by using a corporation. Better yet, don't pay taxes. Your taxes are not being used for your benefit any way. At $10.00 hour, and worked for 30 years you would have paid about $206,000. Now I'm not going to get into things deeper here. But you get my point. $206,000 dollars is only a rough estimate of one person. There are three hundred million people in this country. If there is 300,000,000 people and we all made $10.00 hour that would be $85,714,285.71 million dollars the government would receive. Now, multiply that figure by your imagination. This is based on 3.5 people per house hold.

This is way too much money to end up in any one government. But this does explain why this country is considered a super duper power. It appears we have fed this monster too fat. Those fat cats who live upstairs are responsible.

Let me be a little a less subtle you are nothing but a bottom feeder. From birth to death you are taxed. I cannot count all the ways we are taxed. But I'll give it a try.

Medical tax, employment tax, unemployment tax (poverty tax), nanny tax, student tax, income tax, state tax, federal tax, small business, tax-actors tax, payroll tax, tobacco tax, Indian tax, Canadian tax, energy tax, movie tax, death tax, tea tax, property tax, auto tax, airline tax, estate tax, trader tax, real estate tax, self employment tax, goods and services tax, alternative minimum tax, corporate tax, flat tax tariff and trade tax, proportional tax, progressive tax, repressive tax, progressive tax, social security tax, sin tax, health tax, health care reformation tax, tax on health, marriage tax, divorce tax, capital gains tax, alcohol tax, transfer tax, estimated tax, fiduciary tax, gains tax, hazardous waste tax, highway use fuel tax, pari-mutual tax, petroleum business and fuel excise tax, prompt tax, real estate transfer and mortgage recording tax, sales tax, stock transfer tax, waste tire management tax, wireless communications service tax, forest tax, gas tax, mileage tax, foreclosure tax.

DEFINITION OF TAXES

A tax may be defined as a pecuniary burden lain upon individuals or property to support the government. A tax is not a voluntary payment or donation, but an enforced contribution enacted pursuant to legislative authority and is any contribution imposed by a government whether under a name of toll, tribute, tollage, gabel, impost, duty, custom, excise, aid, supply, or any other name. Taxes consist of direct tax or indirect tax and may be paid in money or labor. Pecuniary means relating to money. So this means taxes are a money burden. When you are born into this country, you automatically inherited a money burden by force. This is because the United States is a corporation. It is said this occurred in the 1930's but forgot to tell everyone.

GOVERNMENTS

A government is an entity. ENTITY-Meaning something with separate existence. This is why governments are called beasts. The beast looks out for it self only. This is the same as self centered. The beast has many things on its mind and has things to accomplish on the world stage. It has eyes every where. Its latest trick is it now can see you through your television screen. The beast is in your computer as well. The beast is smart. He works both sides of the good bad equation. He understands the rules and laws too well. After all he wrote them. The beast runs things like a criminal enterprise. The beast is in the know. He has an agenda to put you in the grave early. He does prolong your death so you can pay him your dues. The beast has in place ways to make your body sickly. He breaks you down daily by poisoning all that you intake from the food you eat to the water you drink.

His agenda is to destroy all that is Godly and natural. Replace it with artificial. He possesses a dual mind set. He pretends to like you but his nature is cold and calculated. The beast has protected our shore line up to this point but this will change. His nature is always problem- reaction- solution. This beast's point of view about humans is low cast slaves.

He is brilliant in creating myths. Creating lies, He knows all the diversion tactics. He has taught all of America's managers their cold blooded ways. Where do you think they learned to be so cold and not care except about that one thing only? You know the money. This beast understands artificial control supply and demand. It creates unseen cartels. It is perfect in performing violence and intimidation. He sits in his deep chamber thinking of ways to sell the public lies and eliminate diversity. After all he has hijacked you and you didn't even know it. He applies back door control. He creates stings.

He now has a plan in place to bring about a nightmare society. In the present day this beast has brought disharmony through the land. It uses the power of the negative. He is at war against your profit. He keeps you low, cast down, unhappy. The beast has introduced the artful language of double speak, and double thing to keep the lie one step ahead of the truth. The beast has 85% of the population dumb down. He feeds you pro feed daily. His long term goal is to destroy peace and freedom.

He will do this by creating war and suffering by chaos and conflict. He has accomplished this and other great feats right in front of you without your knowledge. Or was it with your blessing, either way it's here and now. In the last days this beast will be very popular, and people will love him, but the end will be bitter.

FOODS

Sickness starts by having an acidic body. This means acidic foods. Foods is A wide subject so let me keep it in general. The foods you eat help you feel better. I always feel better after a good meal, don't you? If you put shit in your body then you ate shit. If you ate shit then you have shit in your body it all stands to reason.

Now the body has a job to do. The body's job is to extract what it needs and eliminates the rest. The shit you eat cannot be processed. Therefore it remains inside. The body stores what it cannot eliminate. Now over a period of time this trash gets a build up throughout your system. The result is that you have problems physically. But before your condition appears you will have mental and emotion turmoil going on in your life. All that this means is that something is going inside of you.

Because of this foreign matter in your body you calculate your equations wrong. In other words, you come to wrong conclusions about things. The reason for this is because you are not thinking right. These foreign particles get lodged in your internal organs and remain. You see your liver and kidneys have microscopic holes and these foreign particles get lodged in them which results in them not being able to do there job.

The outward sign of this disharmony is dis-ease. Meanwhile your emotional and mental clarity is diminished. Thereby, dumbing you down, keeping you in the dark. This is one reason your confused, pissed off all the time, angry and can't think straight. I bet your blood is absolutely filthy. If it is dirty, guess what is in it? You guessed it, shit.

Another possibility is that you have parasites. I truly believe everyone has parasites. Where these parasites come from I could not tell you but I'll bet you have them. In fact, I'm sure of it unless you got rid of them knowingly.

What you feed your body also feeds your brain. The reason I know this information is because I too had a few terrible conditions. I made my living as a welder, fabricator. I spent 0ver 30 years breathing toxic fumes that destroyed various parts of my body. It all came to a close quick, but there was signs along the way. I just never paid attention.

My symptoms today are a lot different than they were two years ago. They are of a very personal nature so I will not go into any detail. But I will say this; it will affect me for the rest of my life. My pain became so unbearable. I was moved by desperation to act.

Damned be the doctors. They could not help me any further. I was forced to clean by body inside out. I did not start out with this in mind but I was led along the way and it became part of the process. Let me assure you that detoxing is also painful. Somewhere along the way I acquired a microscope. I began to take notice what was passing through my body. I retrieved these foreign particles and began examining them under the microscope.

What I saw I cannot explain to you in clear detail, But I will say this you will not believe me if I did tell you. It is unexplainable. The medical community will not acknowledge it. Nor will they admit anything. In fact, there is complete denial. I will say this though 'I did observe parasites along the way, various kinds, meaning more than one. I also observed so much crap coming out of my body it is unreal. My body was literally a junk yard.

My pain has subsided, and I am better off as a result of my efforts. Had I not done it I would be in a wheel chair today. As I look back on things I now realize there were signs along the way but I never stopped to examine them. That's not to say I didn't know they were there because I did. I just didn't take them seriously. So I paid the price. This is why I say to you, "You are probably being dumb and stupid right now and not even know or realize it."

Also, remember what you do not put in your body effects you equally, in other words your nutrition or lack thereof. Chances are greater that 90% your body is starving for some kind of nutrient. This means your starving your mind as well. Your body is a very complexes system. It all works in harmony. If one part of it becomes bad then it affects the whole.

People today are totally unhealthy. People cannot see nor think straight because of it. So changing your diet is essential for a healthy body and mind and emotions. It is said your waste line is an indication of your over all health. What is your waste line my friend? If your body is fat and you're a lazy ass you have got a pissed off attitude all the time bitchy, or just a plain old ordinary ass hole then your sick, sick, sick. I bet your to dumb to notice it.

WATER

Blood is the life of the body, and water is the life of the blood. You do have thick and dirty blood. It will remain that way until it isn't that way. The so called water you drink apparently cannot do what it is supposed to do and that is to flush out all the toxins. Our body is sick whether you know it or not just from this water equation alone.

It is said, "You're not sick, you're thirsty." Also, don't treat thirst with medications, but you being dumb and stupid treat your problems with those evil medications (my opinion.)

The city water now-a-days is usually not fit for human consumption. This is why bottled water is so popular. Well water is most generally good but there are wells that are not. Your city water does have chlorine to kill the bacteria. Lime is also added so the pipes don't rust.

While these sources are sustainable for life they are severally inadequate for 100% hydration. Because of this your acidic waste build up keeps building up more causing large problems.

By the way when I was practicing my trade I was sent to a job to tear down a water treatment center in Texas and after that I never looked at city water the same again.

City water is in the neutral range. The ORP in most generally in the higher ORP range than the bottled water. Now remember all diseases stem from the same root cause, A lack of water. Bottled water while it may be a clean source to draw from is acidic. So we have an acidic water source trying to hydrate an acidic body. While water of any kind is better than nothing, these bottled sources are a bit harmful to use. So the question is: "Which one is worse?" There isn't much choice here, is there? ORP means 'Oxidation Reduction Potential'. The higher the positive ORP is, the more acidic the source is. Dasani, a product of Coke, has a positive ORP of about +150. Aquafina, a product of Pepsi, has a positive ORP of about +175. Arrowhead has a positive ORP of about +300. Fiji wellness water has a positive ORP of about +330. Tap water has a positive ORP of about +360. Soda has a positive ORP of about +400.

So tap water is almost as harmful as soda as far as being acidic. To reverse this is to have an ORP to the negative of about -400 of higher. If zero being neutral then a negative would be alkalinity. By drinking alkaline water your body will return or start to return to homeostasis.

Without the alkaline water your body stores your waste as fat and this waste is acidic. This is why you have GERD symptoms among other things. All this to just say your body's chemistry is out of whack. As I said before, your signs are there, but you're not paying attention.

I ask you, are you cranky, moody, angry, or just generally don't feel well in any way? This is nature trying to reach you. The question is, "are you listening?" If not, then you're being stupid.

Our health is determined by 3 influential factors: (1) our genes 20%, (2) our environment 30%, (3) our lifestyle 50%. Disease is caused by a deficiency of oxygen, water, and nutrients. Oxidation equals sickness equals aging.

There are water machines out there that will help you here. They offer (1) Anti-oxidation, (2) Micro clustering, (3) Alkalinity. These machines have the micro cluster technology. What this means is less clustering per molecule (smaller) so the water can better penetrate the cells. Once they can penetrate your cells they can hydrate 100%. Still further after a short time of drinking the water your body will naturally start to detox. Which means it starts flushing all the bad stuff that's making you feel cranky.

Now you must understand that your body has some ungodly stuff in it whether you believe this or not. If you cannot believe this then I will offer this rebuttal only. Next time you see one of those planes in the sky that leaves them long trails then simply retract or reexamine your thinking.

This water is nicknamed miracle water, medical water, Jesus water. Jesus water is holy water. And yes I do have a machine and I definitely drink the water. That's why I know about it. I watch daily as crap is flushed out of my body. It has flushed out iron particles, parasites, infections, which in turn helped my acid reflux. My chronic prostate infection has been reduced. I have experienced some weight loss. And better yet my mind has become clearer.

Today I do not require a doctor. I also take no medications of any kind. Change your water change your life. If you do not believe that your body is filthy then the next time you see an airplane that is leaving all trail behind it then you may rethink your position. Where do you think it ends up?

DRUGS LEGAL & DRUGS ILLEGAL

Let's be real here. Drugs are both good and bad. They have a needed place in our world .My position is this; if you have to plant a seed to make it grow then it can't be all that bad. It is put on earth for us all to be enjoyed. So with that in mind let's move forward.

Opium has been around long before western civilization came to be. China used opium to keep the lower class in there place. Why? Because it keeps them dumb down. Let's face it drugs make you feel better. That's a good thing. Those wonderful people in third world counties grow their drugs and we as Americans buy it. Drugs are very popular. It's reality that sucks. Who do you think buys that opium out of Afghanistan? That's right those in the under ground. Do you think U.S. Government maybe involved a little bit here? I think, why not?

The coca leaf in South America, they have been chewing them leaves long before you and I were born. How about the marijuana plant? Again no harm associated with it. It's how our government is viewing that is more of a problem than anything. Trust me when I say on the outside they are against it while on the inside they wink, wink nod and participate with mucho gusto. Get my drift here.

So the view is, bring it in secretly, control it and the effects it causes. This in turn gives everybody what they want. Those who have control have controlled drugs on the street, money flows every body's happy. Problem is, if you get caught with it you get prison time no questions asked.

Now the legal drugs are what I think are both great and horrendous. We need medicines no doubt there. But what I see coming off of my television screen makes me upset, the advertising of a drug and its benefits on one side of their mouth, while telling you all the bad effects out the other side of their mouth. I heard it said the other day, "An ill for every pill, now there's a pill for every ill." I do believe the health care industry is pushing sickness. Big pharmaceuticals are pushing pills and selling sickness. The world's largest pharmaceutical is looking to turn us all into patients.

We have been conditioned to treat symptoms. Pushing pills is about big pharmaceuticals getting addicted to marketing. They now have tripled there sales people to one sales person to every nine doctors. Boy, talk about the evil genie.

Drugs, like any chemical, keep your vibration low. The more you do them the lower your vibration gets lowered to the point you're weighted down. You spirit gets weighted down and cannot ascend upon your death.

Doing drugs also keeps you from not knowing, unable to become aware, keeps you in your lower place so you cannot rise, keeps you in guilt on top of that. That way you will not question the lies they feed you. They can feed you shit that sounds good, but is not the truth. It is called pro feed.

Drugs create disharmony. Legal drugs bring about social disease. If you are taking them you did so because you were not feeling well. Now you feel better but at your body's expense. But this is only short lived. Is there a conspiracy? I do think there just might be. Pills and bad drugs hasten death. They are slowly killing everyone.

They talk health while creating ill health. Maybe it's back door control. So let's prolong death by speeding it up. Then to make matters worse all that is natural is put asunder. It's all about the money and control. I'll bet there is a conspiracy that is so deep that we dare not mention it here. Drugs screw up your chakras. That's why they push them. Remember the old adage "truth is stranger than fiction."

Because of drugs many people are kept dumb, some remain stupid, and many are broke because of them. Good luck with that. Let me know how that goes. I think EN VOUGE says it best, "FREE YOUR MIND AND THE REST WILL FOLLOW."

THE LAW

The law is the law, is the law. The long arm of the law. The law of the west. I'm sure you've heard all these phrases. I heard it said the other day the only difference between the United States and Russia is that the United States is controlled in secret by few and that Russia is controlled openly by the many. That sounds right to me. Do we need laws? Absolutely. I am all for that. We are a country of over laws, too many rules, too many self centered managers.

We all know what happens when a policeman gets on your tail while you're in your automobile. I personally take a right hand turn immediately, because I know if I do not then I would probably get pulled over for some damn thing. All of you know what I'm talking about here. We can't blame the policeman. They are just doing their job. When they see an infraction they say to them selves there's some revenue for the county.

The biggest area of concentration of evil doers is the county jail. You would think those who get locked up in the county deserve it, while there is truth in it I beg to differ on some points. After ending up there a few times myself I can assure you there are a lot of cases where the defendant is confused about their case. Like getting locked up for not having a drivers license and getting pulled over on their way to work.

When I was thirteen years old, I ran away from home. I took my bow and three arrows a hunting knife a canteen and took off into the desert 40 miles outside of Tucson, around the town of Marana AZ. I spent four days under the hot June sun. I was wearing a tee shirt and a pair of shorts. Now you may not agree with me when I say this was living in the wild. Because it was. My first night I camped on a mountain. Now the howling coyotes run in packs and they were howling all over the desert. It scared me so much I spent half the night in a mesquite tree. Talk about a rough night. After a few nights and days of encountering wild javelinas (mountain pig), rattlers, scorpions, jackrabbits, and sleeping in trees, I came across a small mining town called Silverbell. I was spotted in town at a tiny eatery begging for ham sandwiches. I then wandered out back into the desert. I was picked up on a mining road ten miles out of town.

Now I ran away from home because my situation became intolerable for me. I was emotionally not aware of a lot of things. I was hurting inside. In fact I was sort of dying on the inside. I could not find any people to care for me as a person. I spent my early years crying my self to sleep up to this point. When they found me I was relieved. After them drilling me they wasted no time hauling me to the juvenile lock up. And there I sat in isolation for two weeks.

My crime; walking on a mining road. I did not understand this not one little bit. To this day I am bewildered by it. I did not receive any compassion there. I was not a violent kid nor did I have violent tendencies. They let me go home after two weeks. A few months later I ran away again. I spent one day back up on my desert mountain. My friend rode his horse to come retrieve me. Again I was locked up. For what this time I do not know.

These events occurred in 1973. Since then I have had encountered worse situations, all equally unjust events. My point being here is the law does not care about you or any body else. It cares only for its self preservation. These events were just the introduction of what was to take place along the way. Till this day I am waiting for justice on at least A dozen events. Again, there is no justice from the system in which I have paid my taxes. Lived my life, and even wore a uniform along the way. At every turn I have encountered nothing but cold hearted actions, attitudes, severe punishment for crimes I was not guilty of. Trust me, I could go on. My attitude is this, obey the law when necessary, break the law when you can.

They say crime doesn't pay. I say it does, that's why every politician does it. In retrospect, I should have broken the law, because I paid the price. In recent years blacks have been feeling unjustly punished. I can agree with this. I know this first hand that this is true. But I assure you they are not the only ones being picked on. All males are targeted. It is all part of a larger design. So Through these hardships my point of view is not like yours. I feel like I have been cast into the fire and have been refined. This is why I have encountered many unfortunate souls going through similar experiences. After each and every experience of legal hard ship, I had difficulty in picking my self up and moving on. They kept me in a low place, homeless as a matter of fact. When you're homeless nobody will help unless you're female.

All you spoiled little brats out there I think you need to spend some time in jail. All you women who treat your man like shit ought to spend A few months in solitary. All you politicians need to be lockdown also. I think to be A good lawyer you need to spend A year in lockup. All of these gang members need to be shot, hung till dead. We as A society need to revamp our selves. Clean house. Throw the garbage out. I rest my case. Oh! By the way the town of Silverbell has not even been on the map since I don't know when. Anybody know? Maybe that is justice.

YOUR TIME IS SPENT

Our day to day operations that's the soldier's way. Our daily operations are as follows, morning coffee, kids, food, off to work and school. At work all day put up with all the traffic boss headaches. Bullshit. Come home, laundry, more kids, spouse, food, entertainment.

In addition, our minds are bombarded with more than 8000 subliminal messages per day. Then comes the best part of the day, bedtime. Many people are so troubled that they have bad dreams at night. Are you one of them? Then the next day and we start the same thing all over again. Same shit different day. It ends up being just another day another dollar. Every once in a while we have memorable moments of good or bad happening.

Now, we have more bad feelings running through our veins. Your mind is occupied with the cares of this life. This is the very reason people turn to drugs. Drugs are our way out. What I am trying to convey here is our lives are in a box. There are not too many good choices under this system of things for the common person.

You may not know it but you've been corralled, hoodwinked. Your mind has been numbed, dumbed down, stupefied. You're in your own egg shell. You are unable to see out of it because you're full of chemicals. Your radar screen is malfunctioning. You cannot see the coming events. But, you can feel it. You know it's there. You are in suspended darkness and you don't' even know it and some don't even care.

While your mind is in darkness the evil genies slip in and out of obscurity like shadows. You can't see them because you have this blurred vision. You spend your time at everything in the world except on those who are behind this mess. How can you anyway. They are obscure. With all this going on you have A hard time taking care of your self. Most of you cannot properly do it. There is not enough time in the day to properly give attention to all of these events, much less take care of them. So we make our decisions and hope for the best. Sometimes they work out and sometimes they don't. This is the reason people make bad choices.

Another reason is that they are not mentally disciplined. Too much is happening all around you. In fact, there is so much happening all around you that you cannot see anything else but those things. Take a step back from all things and watch the gods at work. Once you tune your frequency into this station only can you start to see all the happenings around you. The gods are at work behind the scene. You can't always see them because there are many and they have different personalities. They do not appear to be evil. But they are there, and they are in control.

To make matters worse you will never be able to see him because to do so you have to start being honest with your self on a deep level and you probably can't do that because your to dumb. You are too far gone. So out of this I say get off your damn medications, get off of your fat ass and stay away from me. Open up your damn mind and quit being such a dumb ass. Keep your big mouth shut. Get away from that bitch your with or that ass hole your married to. Life is to short to be putting up with their bullshit. All they do is rob you of your life. They strip away your life day by day. Fire your boss. And tell him exactly how you feel and I mean let him have it. Don't hold back anything. Remember there is no such thing as wrong feelings. All this shit you put up with is life draining anyway. The gods are at work to bring this system to a close.

The time to go out and live is now. Don't believe what your eyes see. Nothing is as it seems anyway. We are on shaky ground. Quit looking at what you don't like and start looking at what you want. Work on your self making your life happier. Go get some ice cream. Then go find a wild piece of ass. See, things are looking better already. Learn to live in real time. Your power is in the now. Live like yesterday doesn't matter and it won't. Make your presence felt. Send your negatives vibes back into space where they belong. There are more negative thoughts on the earth than the sand on the sea shore. Remember if it is not good for your organism then it's not good for you. I rest my case. I'll see you in the future.

MIND DISEASE

Mind set of a loser: Create a problem, agitate the problem, then have problem with anybody who has a problem with it. All I can say is welcome to the jungle.

Does this sound like somebody you know? I bet is does. I was married to two of them. They are always conjuring up problems that are not real. They are imagined only. They used their power to conjure them into reality. This is the problem with relationships today. The mystical mind set is the natural mind in the disease mode.

Conjure means: 1. summon by sorcery. 2. Practice by sleight of hand. 3. Entreat. This is a phenomenon that is an epidemic. It happens in relationships between two people in all aspects of human endeavor. I see it everyday in just about every situation. Sleight of hand means to let loose a non truth as though it is truth. This is other wise known as a non sequitur.

How about this? It is making a problem where none previously existed. It is turning that which was right upside down and made it wrong. Another example is this, taking a nice brand new home and trashing it. Or better yet, having a beautiful landscape in the Oregon country and converting it into a junk yard trash dump. I have seen this first hand. If I say anything about it then they think me a wrong thinker. Talk about upside down. Talk about sick. Talk about a disease.

Another example: I see so many people nowadays with chemical altered bodies. They are so out of whack that they cannot walk. They look absolutely hideous. This goes to my ex-spouses as well. They just let their life go to shit. They have an inability to care for their self. You try to care for them in your own way and they think you are punishing them. They cannot stand you because you have a better view of health. And you actually lead the way with your healthy lifestyle. Then they divorce you thinking that they are right all along. Meanwhile you have no health issues at all and they have multiple serious health issues. This is the disease I am talking about. Can you see it? The above examples are my ex-wife and in-laws. I lasted in this relationship for 14 years. So I know first hand this devastating mind set. I introduced health conscious ideas to this family and they vehemently rejected everything. I brought to them alkalized water to fruits and vegetables.

So I now can only say to them. Listen I am sorry, I did not want to take away your wonderful disease from you. I now see that you are happy with your conditions. I had no idea that you have a great relationship with your wheel chair. I was of the understanding you would like to live a little longer. Perhaps you were right all along, your time on this earth should be cut short. Good bye. Can you see the two mind sets? They are opposite one another.

I think Jesus said it best when He stated that you will know them by their fruits. You will know them by what they do.

Here is another example: I used to hang around the Jehovah's witnesses. I thought I would just try an experiment and see if this is where I belong. My older dear friend invited me so I went. I decided to become a regular member. After doing so for some time I thought everything was ok. Once in a while I would lightly touch some one as we all would normally do in a respectful way. One year later some one had a problem with this. But since it wasn't a problem they forgot to bring it to me until six months after the fact. I thought this strange. Now it is a problem.

They called me into the back room to nicely chide me. I called them on it. They were evasive. I brought them to the knowledge that no sin was committed. They ignored my statements. I spoke to them the word of God, they hung their heads in denial. They were committed to making me voluntarily submit to their nice accusations. I refused submission. I reminded them that we are all brothers and that they were accusing me of something that did not exist. Again they hung their heads to hide the scales over their eyes. I then told them that I have slain the dragon of accusations. They did not understand what I was trying to convey. I left never to go back unless I occupy the pulpit. Again that will never happen.

As I pondered about this troubling issue I realized slowly I had been set up by my old dear friend. This man is 67 years old. He was not happy that I was going my own way and he was angry he had spent so much time investing in me only for me to walk away. So he set up a mild sting. He accused me of false things. He made statements that I could read between the lines. This is how I found out it was him that set me up. I reminded him of his sin. He refused to listen. I then told him about the upside down human nature. He walked away in denial. I also reminded him that I am an equal and not subservient. He just shook his head and said that I just don't get it. Now you tell me what is wrong with this picture.

I tell you this story because this is the latest one I have encountered. There are many, many more that I could share. In the eyes of God he has made his brother stumble. I was extremely disturbed after this. I did not understand what I had done that was wrong and how it can be viewed as sin. The only answer is the mind disease, this man had posed as a friend and worked as a con, simple as that.

I said to this man that I think this is God's way of pulling me out of your midst. He stated that it was the devil who was doing it. I just shook my head and said nothing. The end.

The evil mind set is a social disease that is an epidemic. People are always slapping you down with subliminal messages. They are in their own egg shell and cannot escape. This person above in question has a very messy house. He does have health issues. He does have a questionable marriage. He does have his own problems. So he is just human. But he is unaware of his mind disease.

The affects of this dis-ease are all around us everywhere. The apostle Paul touches base on this subject when he talks about the flesh. The flesh is malice, strife, disorder, hateful comments. Basically it is the upside down of human nature. This is what I will call the nature of the dragon.

This is the nature of the dragon instilled in humans to do the will of the dragon to the ends of the world. It is specifically designed to bring this old world to a destructive and violent end. Guess what that is exactly what is coming about, is it not?

False accusations are the human being putting God to the test. False accusations are you mocking God. God states in return that He will not be mocked. It is the lying to the Holy Spirit that is unforgivable. This is a great sin! There are always repercussions of it in our lives. It is sin but it also is an energy issue. Whatever it is that you sow that is what you will reap is the rule. Religious or not they apply to us all.

I am touching base with the dark side of human nature. This is the side that we all know that is there but do not talk about it do to its uncomfortable nature. We are all fight with this mind set. We are all struggling with it. It plagues us daily all day long and will never leave us alone. This is why I sit here today at the age of 52 writing about this. I have had a life time of seeing and experiencing this in my life.

I could give example after example. I am addressing it at this time because I can see that the wall of right and wrong has been blurred. The thin layer of keeping it together or letting it come forward. People are starting to be very rude in business and not realize it. This disease is flowing into business. Traditionally this is where it stops, but not anymore.

This is the social dis-ease that destroys our relationships. It destroys our cities, and it is destroying our country. You cannot make things better unless you first admit that you have a problem. Will it get better? Absolutely not! So brace your self for what is about to come in the future.

This essay right here is a warning. I am trying to bring your attention to this issue. It is food for thought. Look upon your self and see what damage you have caused. Yes! You! Chances are 95% you are a major cause of your house hold being torn apart. This is you that is the problem. You know what I'm talking about here.

I see your mind disease. I have suffered under it. Now I am master over it. Got it? I see you in all your ways. Your mystical mind set and your twisted ways I see it fully now. People like you that have made my life miserable. You have taught me that doing the right thing was all wrong. You are not worthy of my labor any longer. I cannot cherish you any longer either. I cannot even talk to people like you for fear of false prosecution. You have also taught me not to care. Shall I go on? Your mind is in a black fog.

In public I see the walls go up. Hell! I have mine up. I am no different here. But at least I am aware of it. We all have brick walls around us. We put them there for protection, protection against what exactly? So we don't get hurt by other people. The point here is that we are hurting each other with our social dis-ease. Are we not a civil society? Not for long. We are breaking down, but that is another matter.

I think the main reason for this dis-ease is stagnation. Our lives are humdrum and we lack excitement. We have life sucking lives and jobs. We are also in stagnant relationships. We are coming to the edge of our dark lives and are unable to take much more as humans. Time is just about ripe for people to rebel. So I am not here to stop this. I am here talking to you about this issue to make known and then to facilitate in humble service. I am all for what ever makes you happy. Be it peace or chaos. Cheat to win and win to cheat. Lie to gain. Gain and lie.

Rules are there to be broken. Rules are more like guidelines anyhow. Rules are there only for the stupid and simple. Truly there are not any rules, right?

The mind dis-ease is responsible for all wars, planet destroying, all dis-harmony between individuals. All discords between nations. It is responsible for all divorces, strife, riots, and chaos.

Now get this it is natural that is why we naturally do it. We are geniuses at it. We were born to lose. We were born to screw things up. So I think nature got it wrong. No wonder God repented to all of heaven when He created man. This smacks right into sin being in our DNA.

This dragon is in our DNA. We are unable to do anything about it. Not on our own anyhow. This is also known as our mystical mind set. This is why it has caused so much destruction. All these things I say are right in front of you all you have to do is stop and look at it.

The dragon is a deity that is not here as of yet. But don't worry, he is on his way. I can here his voice. I can feel him in the air. I can see him in you. His nature is in you, you just don't know it. That is why when he comes you will embrace him. He will be a cool cat I can say that. He will be very popular as well. He will also be some one that you don't want to get on the bad side of or else, off with your head.

This deity has a purpose. Its purpose is to cut your life short by any means necessary. It gives you everything you desire, all you have to do is serve it. But at the same time it will poison you. Give you medication that is not good for you. It lies to you and keeps you in the dark. It side tracks you in every possible way so as to keep his agenda secret. It has created diseases in your body. It has conjured up massive mental disease. It has brought to you all social rottenness. It has chemically altered your once beautiful body. It has done nothing but lie to your mind about who you really are. It has saved you from Almighty God. It does love you and has plans to be with you in eternity. It has promised you everything you could ever want falsely.

Shall I reverse this? It has reshaped your body to its image. The body God gave you at birth was bad. The fat barrel shape you have now is the right one. The healthy body at birth was wrong. Your diseased one is the right path now. This is why you have it, right? The loving child that you once were is wrong. The ass hole and bitch is the real you, right? The openness of life that we all had as children and the zeal for life is now replaced with fear, worry and massive self doubt. Now we are talking real passion hear, right? Instead of desiring a better here and now we have replaced it with hell on earth. This is our course. Get it? I desire not to spend my eternity in peaceful heaven I want to spend it in hell. After all there is no sex in heaven. No Harley Davidson roadways there, or is there? No copulation going on in heaven, right, or is there?

This is called irrational. Doesn't make much sense, does it? But this is our thinking nevertheless. Irrationality is the energy behind all wars and diseases and destructive emotions. But being lost souls we don't know better. We rationalize our bad behavior. Maybe this is why Jesus said "forgive them Father for they do not know what it is they do," while they were nailing Him to the cross.

Oh! by the way, the Jehovah's witnesses believe that Jesus was not nailed to a cross but a single post instead. I like the cross idea better myself.

Being stupid humans we are constantly using our diseased against one another with stupid accusations that are just plain dumb. We are cunning to one another. We use deception towards one another. There by practicing the law of the jungle. May the fittest survive, so much for peace on Earth. Lying is said to be witchcraft. Lying is the real witchcraft.

Out of these real life experiences I look at life radically different these days. First off nothing is what it seems. Next my eyes may see, but they always doubt. There is reality then there is false reality.

Reality is best defined as all those things that are life giving to my organism, healthy for mind, body and soul. False reality is best defined as not good for my organism. But it gives excitement to ego which is the false self. This is of course brings non living to life.

No longer do I see religion as the final answer. Nor do I trust religious people all the time. Truth is they are more trust worthy as those who are not. Then again an enemy is always trust worthy in the fact they will not lie to you. An enemy will tell straight up because he has no cause to lie. They are indeed intertwined.

My job was not real in the fact it was not good for my organism. It put money in my account no doubt there. But it was a hostile work place like all seem to be nowadays.

I am not a man after God's own heart. I am leaning more of being a god after man's own wallet. Hey! Nothing personal, just doing business. I no longer look at women as something to be cherished. I now look at them as hideous creatures that are very nice looking and can't live without. In my view the devil wears a dress and has tits and blue eyes. If it has tits or wheels you are going to have problems with it.

So there is reality and then there is false reality. False reality is the reality we live in that brings all strife, malice, hateful gestures, and the subliminal slapping we give one another. It is the point of the compass that head to all progress south, south to be meaning all hell on earth. What do you say that we together make hell on earth a little better for one another? Do this for me, Please!

How about another story for good measure! This is true you know. I got this girl pregnant. She was very cute, loved her dimples. I thought it the right thing to marry. After all we were going to have a family.

First mistake, I followed my belief system. I had nothing but relationship problems right away. She did all sorts of things that were not normal. Like sleep in her car because she got mad and then caught sick. I will spare you the details. After the baby was born she began accusing me of all sorts on nonsense. Me being a hard working man trying to make a future was about to learn some lessons. She put me to school in deception. When I first met her she pretended to have this ailment so she put her self in the hospital. The doctors could not find what was wrong. This was my first clue. But I did not learn well enough. Well! She did this thing again in other ways. But things escalated and then went diverse. Talk about my head spinning and confused. It took me awhile to figure things out because not one thing made sense. False accusations did stick at this time. Then later as I tried to avoid her It got worse. She would call The State troopers and accused me of horrible things. Well, this was the beginning of the end for her illusions. It just took a little time. The elapsed time from beginning to end was about 7 years. I had endured 7 years of pure hell. What was my crime? To this day I do not know except that she must have been my only crime. My innocent self was my undoing.

So this subject in question about the upside down thinking, this is my new domain. I have been schooled in hard reality of non reality. Is it real? Hell yes! It was real. But it all was the world of unreal. Get my point. So don't think me here as delusional. I have learned the fine art of non reality verses reality. No one more than I can explain it better, unless of course you can. I tell you what. Do you have a story for me? I would like to hear it. Put pen to paper and write it down. I would love to read it.

So were did she end up? Glad you asked. She took a dirt nap. Don't ask me how because I do not know the answer to that question. I just know that I was reading the newspaper one day always expecting to see her in the obituaries. Then Bam! Shazam! One day there she was, dead. Shall I say God rest her soul, or god damn her soul? Either way the earth was purged. Good riddance.

Then I saw the same signs emerging in my second relationship. I watched over a period of 14 years her symptoms getting worse. I did not let things get out of hand this time. My second wife was a defeated foe from the beginning. To this day she does not admit it. She is in false reality. Her world is quickly deteriorating. But I cannot save her. For 14 years I have tried but have failed. She just cannot see it for the life of her. I pity the woman fool. She is now woe-man. She is self destructing in the mind body and her environment. It is a matter of time. She is closing the gap between living on top of the earth versus under the earth. These people all practiced the mystical mind set with little success.

ERNEST JOHNSON

A WELDER AND HIS DISEASE

My name is Ernest Johnson and for the last four years eight months I have worked for Johnson Crushers Inc. I was a welder in crusher bay. I worked the swing shift without any supervision during my time there. There wasn't any need for a supervisor. A supervisor would not know anything about my job anyway. Each person is his own specialist. Each employee is a highly trained professional. I received my daily instructions from the guys on the floor. They are the ones that trained me. They have been my mentors. They are the true heroes in this story.

Then one day a new supervisor was appointed. A big headed machinist named Darrel Strawn. He had arguments with everybody. He stuck his nose in every body's business. He also made a few high profile mistakes of his own. He one day stuck his nose in my business and tried to change a welding process. I told him no. He put an untrained man on it anyway. He wanted to use three welding guns on a one gun flat only position. I told him this was a no no. From an engineering stand point it is a no no. I argued with him and I got fired. So much for doing the right thing.

This man does not know my job. He does not know the first thing about my job. His new found power was without limits. Where were the do right mangers now? Hiding that's where.

The managers at JCI are all about anti employee. They wear two faces and they are opposites. One manager named Mr. Johnson, head of human resources is strictly a head hunter. Nothing good there. They are self centered. They do not look out for their employees. They care only about increasing their own power. JCI managers have no JCI value. They are so lazy they will not make the necessary changes on their prints. I once joked with co-workers I could have went to college got my degree in engineering, got a job in the office and made the necessary changes on the shop prints faster than they could do it. Talk about pathetic.

At JCI the air quality is so poor, visibility is in question. The air is totally toxic. After ten hours of day shift welding, swing shift comes in and has another 10 hours to add to it. Then add in a dozen machinists and their toxic substance. What have you got? You get the picture. The air could not in no way pass OSHA.

Crusher bay has six 800lb spools of 3/32 wire sitting there. Eight welders and as many four to five welders going, many at the same time. In addition there is a lot of air arcing going on. Not to mention grinding dust. (grinding wheels have fibers). So what we have here is a toxic soup mix of Welding and grinding fibers along with copper and carbon with iron particles. Then add a mixture of Machinist burning liquid from a dozen machines or so and you have a very poisoning environment. It stays that way all day and all night. They are anti opening the door. Most often it is a closed environment.

After a year or so I started having problems with my prostate. My reproduction system was under going a bad change. My semen became discolored. The texture also became stringy. It was being destroyed. I encountered erectile disfunction. This sprung me into action.

I had come down with a urinary tract infection. A bladder infection. An infected prostate. My kidney's were at 57% capacity. This is kidney disease. It burned every time I urinated. It burned every time I ejaculated. I had cystitis. My seminal tubes were also infected. I was being poisoned daily. My groin was on fire. I could hardly walk. The pain was excruciating. It was non stop for the next three years.

During this trying time I found the strength to show up and work and never did wussy out. Meanwhile I sought medical help but was rewarded little. During the next three years I put it all together. I began to pay attention a little bit more day in and day out. Slowly I began to realize that It was my environment that was the cause of my illness.

I sought medical help. It only got me to antibiotics. This did little. Now remember I am in a lot of pain. In desperation I made a call to some one who had some prostate cleanse. I found relief almost immediately. Also I was introduced to another herbal remedy called detox. This stuff is like gasoline, but it is miraculous.

Once on the prostate cleanse and the detox I began to flush out little black specks. I fished them out and took them to my urologist. They determined them to be concentration. In real time they were microscopic fibers. A little ball of fiber. Now they did hurt when they came out. Then came the full body cleanses.

Next I did a kidney/bladder cleanse. That's when all the mucus and fibers came pouring out. After that I did a liver/gallbladder cleanse. More of the same thing. The nastiest looking film came out. After wards I continued with the prostate cleanse and the detox. The detox is a kidney, blood, bladder herbal formula. It accomplished the impossible. It did what the doctors could not do. The doctors would not even go there. They showed me denial, disbelief. I swear I pissed a five gallon bucket of fibers. I say piss on them doctors.

I am not completely well of it yet. My body has took a terrible hit. I will forever be altered in body and mind. I consider it my awakening. Remember welders, your maleness is holy ground. Your prostate is holy.

LONG TERM (CHRONIC) OVER EXPOSURE EFFECTS

Welding fumes-Excess levels may cause bronchial asthma, lung fibrosis, pneumoconiosis or "siderosis. "

Bronchial-Bronchi- The two main branches leading from the Trachea to the lungs. Providing the passageway for air movement. The presence of any foreign material in the bronchi may cause various diseases. Foreign bodies usually are aspirated into the right bronchi.

Asthma-A disease caused by increased responsiveness of the tracheobronchial tree to various stimuli.

Bronchial Asthma-Allergic asthma. Common form of asthma due to hypersensitivity to an allergen. The result is paroxysmal constriction of the bronchial aiarwaves. Clinically, there is severe dyspnea accompanied by wheezing.

Dyspnea-Breathing. Air hunger resulting labored or difficult breathing, SYM: Audible labored breathing. Distressed anxious expression, dilated nostrils, protrusion of abdomen and expanded chest, gasping marked cyanosis.

Cyanosis-Insufficient oxygenation of the blood resulting from disturbances in the lungs, low oxygen pressure of air. Circulatory disturbances, hemoglobin deficiency. Other causes may be Acidosis, excessive $co2$ content of blood, lesions of the Respiratory center, emotional excitation, hyper excitability of Hering-Brever reflex, cardiac asthma and orthopnea. It may be a subjective feeling.

Acidosis-Excessive acidity of body fluids due an accumulation of acids or an excessive loss of bicarbonate (as in renal disease). The hydrogen ion concentration.

Lung Fibrosis-Formation of scar tissue in connective tissue frame work of the lungs following inflammation or pneumonia and in pulmonary tuberclulosis.

Pneumoconiosis-A condition of the respiratory tract due to inhalation of dust particles. An occupational disorder such as that caused by mining, stonecutting, or welding.

Siderosis- SYN Welders disease. A form of pneumoconiosis resulting from inhalation of dust or fumes containing particles. See hemosiderosis.

Hemosiderosis-Condition characterized by the deposition, esp. in liver and spleen, of hemosiderin occurs In diseases in which there is marked red cell destruction such as hemolytic anemias, pernicious anemia and chronic infection. See: Hemochromatosis.

Iron, Iron oxide fumes-Can cause Siderosis(deposits of iron in lungs) which some researchers believe may affect pulmonary function. Lungs will clear in time when exposure to iron and its compounds ceases. Iron and magnetite ($f3o4$) are not regarded as fibrogenic materials.

Fibro-Fiber combining form fibrous matter or structure.

-Genic-Pertaining to production or generation.

Manganese-Long term exposure to manganese compounds may effect the central nervous system. Symptoms may be similar to Parkinson's disease and can include slowness, changes in handwriting, gait impairment, muscle spasms and cramps and less commonly, tremor and behavioral changes. Employees who are over exposed to manganese compounds should be seen by a physician for early detection of neurologic problems. See psychiatry.

Neurologic-Reason, pertaining to the study of nervous diseases.

Central nervous system-Brain and spinal cord, with their nerves and end organs that control voluntary and involuntary acts. Includes parts of the brain governing consciousness and mental activities; Parts of the brain, spinal cord, and their sensory and motor nerve fibers controlling skeletal muscles; and end organs of the body. Comp: nerve tissue that forms the brain, spinal cord, and the nerves from both. Tissue is made of gray and white matter. Gray matter is composed of cells of nerve tissue. While the white matter is composed of nerve fibers from the cells. White matter in the brain and cord carries a message or impulses from the body or outside world to the cells or gray matter.

Parkinson's disease-A chronic nervous disease characterized by a fine, slowly spreading tremor, muscular weakness and rigidity, and a peculiar gait.

Titanium Dioxide-Pulmonary irritation and slight fibrosis.

Fibrosis-Condition. Abnormal formation of fibrous tissue. F. of lungs. Formation of scar tissue framework of lungs following inflammation or pneumonia and in pulmonary tuberculosis.

Silica (Amorphous)- research indicates that silica is present in welding fume in the amorphous form. Long term overexposure may cause pneumoconiosis. Non crystalline forms of silica (amorphous silica) are considered to have little fibrotic potential.

Amorphous-without form. (smoke)

Fibrotic-Marked by or pert. To fibrosis.

Pneumoconiosis-A condition of the respiratory tract due to inhalation of dust particles an occupational disorder such as that caused by welding.

Fluorides-Serious bone erosion (osteoporosis) and mottling of teeth.

Osteoporosis-Condition. A general term for describing any disease process that results in reduction in the mass of bone per unit of volume. The reduction is sufficient to interfere with the mechanical support of bone. The term does not indicate a specific etiological agent; indeed, many conditions and diseases may be involved in the process. The bones that are more frequently involved are the vertebrae of the lower dorsal and lumbar areas. Osteoporosis may effect any bone, including the jaw.

Mottling-Many colored. Condition that is marked by discolored areas.

Molybdenum-Prolonged over exposure may result in loss of appetite, weight loss, loss of muscle coordination, difficulty in breathing and anemia.

Anemia-A reduction in the number of circulating red blood cells per cu mm. The amount of hemoglobin per 100ml, or the volume packed red blood cells per 100mls of blood. Anemia is not a disease; it is a symptom of various diseases.

Etiol: Anemia may result from excessive blood loss, excessive blood cell destruction, or decreased cell formation. Anemia due to excessive blood loss results from acute or chronic hemorrhage. Anemia due to excessive blood cell destruction occurs in hemolytic disease or hypersplenism.

Calcium Oxide-Prolonged overexposure may cause ulceration of the skin and perforation of the nasal septum, dermatitis and pneumonia

Ulceration-Suppuration occurring on a free surface, as on the skin or on a mucus membrane.

Perforation- The act or process of making a hole, such as caused by ulceration. The hole made through a substance or part.

Dermatitis-Inflammation of the skin evidenced by itching, redness, and various skin lesions.

Pneumonia-Inflammation of the lungs caused primarily by bacteria, viruses, and chemical irritants. There are more than 50 causes.

Aluminum Oxide-Pulmonary fibrosis and emphysema.

Pulmonary Fibrosis-Fibrosis of the lung following any pulmonary disease. Condition. Abnormal formation of fibrous tissue. F. of lungs. Formation of scar tissue in connective tissue framework of lungs following inflammation of pneumonia in pulmonary tuberculosis.

Emphysema-To inflate. Pathological distention of tissue by gas or air in the interstices. A chronic pulmonary disease characterized by increase beyond the normal in the size if air spaces distal to the terminal bronchiole with destructive changes in their walls. Syn. Chronic obstructive pulmonary disease; Pulmonary emphysema.

Magnesium, Magnesium Oxide-No adverse long term health effects have been reported in the literature.

Barium-Long term over exposure to soluble barium compounds may cause nervous disorders and may have deleterious effects on the heart, circulatory system, and musculature.

Disorders-Pathological condition of the mind or body. See disease.

Deleterious-Harmful.

Circulatory system-The cardiovascular system consisting of the heart and blood vessels (arteries, arterioles, capillaries, venules, veins, and sinuses) and the lymphatic system.

Musculature-The arrangement of muscles in the body or its parts.

Nickel, Nickel compounds-Lung fibrosis or pneumoconiosis. Some studies of nickel refinery workers indicated a higher incidence of lung and nasal cancers.

Lung fibrosis- Formation of scar tissue in connective tissue framework of lungs following inflammation or pneumonia and in pulmonary tuberculosis.

Pneumoconiosis- A condition of the respiratory tract due to inhalation of dust particles. An occupational disorder such as that caused by mining, or welding.

Chromium-Ulceration and perforation of nasal septum. Respiratory irritation may occur with systems resembling asthma. Studies have shown that chromate production workers exposed to hexavalent chromium compounds have an excess of lung cancers. Chromium 6 compounds are more readily absorbed through the skin than chromium3 compounds. Good practice requires the reduction of employee exposure to chromium3 and 6 compounds.

Hexavalent-(to have power) Having a chemical valence of six. SYN: sexivalent.

Valence-(powerful) Property of an atom or group of atoms causing them to combine in definite proportion with other atoms or groups of atoms. Valency may be as high 8 and is determined by the number of electrons in the outer orbit of the atom. Degree of the combining power or replacing power of an atom or group of atoms, the hydrogen atom being the unit of comparison. The number indicates how many atoms of hydrogen can unit with one atom of another element.

Copper-Copper poison has been reported in the literature from exposure to high levels of copper. Liver damage can occur due to copper accumulating in the liver characterized by cell destruction and cirrhosis. High levels of copper may cause anemia and jaundice. High levels of copper may cause central nervous system damage characterized by nerve fiber separation and cerebral degeneration.

Cerebral-Pert. To the cerebrum. The cerebrum is the largest portion of the brain, consisting of two hemispheres separated by a deep longitudinal fissure. The hemispheres are united by three commissures. The corpus callosum and the anterior and posterior hippocampus commissures. The surface of each hemisphere is thrown into numerous folds or convolutions called gyri, which are separated by furrows called fissure or sulci.

Phys-The cerebrum is concerned with sensations or the interpretation of sensory impulses; and all voluntary muscular activities. It is the seat of consciousness and the center of the higher mental faculties such as memory, learning, reasoning, judgment, intelligence, and the emotions.

On the basis of function, several areas have been identified and located. Among them are motor projection areas, which give rise to fibers carrying efferent impulses to effecter organs, the skeletal muscles; sensory projection areas; which receive impulses from sense organs or sensory receptors by way of the brain stem, including the so esthetic (visual, auditory, gustatory, and olfactory) areas; and association areas, which are concerned with the higher mental faculties.

Degeneration-Deterioration or impairment of an organ or part in structure of cells and the substances of which they are a part.

Jaundice-Condition characterized by yellowness of skin. Whites of eyes, mucus members, and body fluids due to deposition of bile pigment resulting from excess bilirubin in the blood.

Bilirubin-The orange colored or yellowish pigment in bile. It is carried to the liver by the blood.

Cirrhosis-A chronic disease of the liver characterized by formation of dense per lobular connective tissue, degenerative changes in parenchyma cells, alteration in stricture of chords of liver lobules, fatty and cellular infiltration, and sometimes development of areas of regeneration. In addition to the clinical signs and symptoms inherent in the cause of cirrhosis, those due to cirrhosis are the result of loss of functioning liver cells and increased resistance to flow of blood through the liver (portal hypertension). When severe enough, leads to ammonia toxicity.

Anemia-A reduction in the number of circulating red blood cells. See Above.

Central Nervous System-Brain and spinal cord, with their nerves and end organs that control voluntary and involuntary acts. Includes parts of the brain governing consciousness and mental activities; parts of the brain, spinal cord, and their sensory and motor nerve fibers controlling skeletal muscles; and end organs of the body. Comp. Nerve tissue that forms the brain, spinal cord, and the nerves from both. Tissue is made of gray matter. Gray matter is composed of cells of nerve fibers from the cells. White matter in the brain and cord carries a message or impulse from the body or outside world to the cells or gray matter.

Cells- A small enclosed or partly enclosed cavity such as an air cell. A mass of protoplasm containing a nucleus or nuclear material. It is the unit of structure of all animals and plants. Cells and the products of cells make up all the tissues of the body.

Destructive-Causing ruin or destruction. Opposite of construction.

Strontium Compounds-Strontium at high doses is known to concentrate in bone. Major signs of chronic toxicity, which involve the skeketon, have been labeled as "strontium rickets".

Chronic- Of long duration. Designating a disease showing little change or of slow progress. Opposite of acute.

Toxicity-The extent, quality, or degree of being poisonous.

Strontium- A dark yellow metal. Medically it is of interest because it's radioactive isotope. 90sr constitutes a radioactive hazard in fallout from atom bombs. The isotope has a half-life of 28 years and is stored in bone when ingested.

Rickets-A deficiency condition in children that results in inadequate deposition of lime salts in developing cartilage and newly formed bone, causing abnormalities in shape and structure of bones. SYN:Osteomalacia, rachitis.

Skeleton-The bony framework of the body consisting of 206 bones.

Lithium Compounds-May be considered as potentially teratogenic.

Teratogenic-(generation, birth). Concerning spermatogenesis.

Teratogenesis-The development of abnormal structures in an embryo resulting in a severely deformed fetus.

Osteomalacia-A disease marked by increasing softness of the bones, so that they become flexible and brittle, thus causing deformities. Osteomalacia is the adult form of rickets. Systems: Rheumatic pains in the limbs, spine, thorax, and esp. the pelvis; anemia and signs of deficiency or loss of calcium salts due to vitamin d deficiency.

Rachitis-Inflammation of the spine. Rickets

Cobalt-Repeated over exposure to cobalt compounds can produced reduced pulmonary function, diffuse nodular fibrosis of lungs and respiratory hypersensitivity. IARC considers cobalt compounds as possibly carcinogenic to humans.

Diffuse-spreading, scattered, spread.

Nodular- a small node. A small aggregation of cells.

Fibrosis-Abnormal formation of fibrous tissue of lungs. Formation of scar tissue in connective tissue framework of lungs following inflammation or pneumonia and in pulmonary tuberculosis.

Respiratory system-The organs involved in the interchange of gases between an organism and the atmosphere. In the human, it consists of the nose, pharynx, larynx, trachea, bronchi, and lungs. Breathing.

Hypersensitivity- Abnormal sensitivity at a stimulus of any kind.

Carcinogenic-Producing cancer.

Cystitis.Inflammation of the bladder usually occurring secondary to ascending urinary tract infections. Associated organs (kidney, prostate, urethra) may be involved. May be acute or chronic.

LIST OF KNOWN DISEASE

1. Bronchial Asthma
2. Lung Fibrosis

3. Siderosis or pneumoconosis
4. Central Nervous System
5. Parkinson's Disease
6. Slight Fibrosis
7. Osteoporosis
8. Emphysema
9. Circulatory System
10. Lung and nasal cancers
11. Asthma
12. Cell Destruction
13. Anemia
14. Jaundice
15. Fiber Separation
16. Chronic Toxicity
17. Cerebral Degeneration
18. Skeleton Softening
19. Rickets
20. Cancer
21. Dermatitis
22. Pneumonia
23. Tremors
24. Osteomalacia
25. Teeth discoloration
26. Acidosis
27. Birth defects
28. Erectile dysfunction
29. Blood Poisoning
30. Dyspnea
31. Hemisiderious
32. Pulmonary Disorders
33. Lung Fibrosis
34. Ulceration
35. Perforation
36. Atom Destruction
37. Nervous Disorders
38. Portal Hypertension

39. Rheumatic.
40. Hypersensitivity
41. Seminal Vesiculitis
42. Acid Reflux
43. Cystitis
44. Urinary Tract Infection
45. Prostate Infection
46. Kidney Disease
47. Bladder Infection

LIST OF KNOWN SYMPTOMS

1. Discomfort
2. Dizziness
3. Nausea
4. Dryness
5. Chills
6. Irritation
7. Fever
8. Upset Stomach
9. Vomiting
10. Aching Body
11. Skin Burns
12. Eye Burns
13. Edema
14. Bronchitis
15. Metal Taste
16. Tightness of Chest
17. Aching Eyes
18. Rhinitis
19. Frontal Headache
20. Wheezing
21. Laryngeal Spasms
22. Salivation
23. Anorexia
24. Metal Fume Fever
25. Allergic Reaction

26. Lung Damage
27. Asthma Like Systems
28. Severe Injury of death
29. Ulcers
30. Gastrointestinal Disorders
31. Tremors
32. Coughs
33. Weight Loss
34. Pulmonary Irritation

SKULL AND CROSS BONES

Where there is welding there are welding fumes. The welding fumes are the smoke. It is in an amorphous state (without definite form). In this amorphous state are tiny particles. These particles have microscopic fibers. These fibers are what are toxic. These fibers come in many colors. These are what will destroy your body and mind. They are extremely toxic to every part of your being, from head to toe.

These microscopic fibers enter the workers body through the eyes, skin, and primarily through the breathing which is the nose and mouth. Once into the lungs the damage starts. They work through the lungs to the workers pulmonary system. These fibers do not remain there. They move on into other parts of the body. They travel to the outside of your internal organs. Where ever they land they poison.

Your kidneys and liver are porous, they find there way into these two organs. They infiltrate these organs and toxicify them. Once in these organs they eventually enter the blood stream. Once in the blood stream they travel through the blood stream throughout the entire body. Every thing they touch they poison. It does so in subtle ways over a period of time.

The longer the worker is exposed to these fumes the more fibers enter their body; the more fibers that enter the body the greater the toxicity. Toxicity is poison.

They travel to the very depths of the human body. At first internal inflammation occurs. Then that inflammation turns into damaged organs. It will eventually shut down the workers organs. Great damage to the workers reproductive system also occurs.

Your liver and kidneys are microscopic porous. They can store microscopic particles thus creating Cirrhosis of the liver and kidney disease. The blood becomes more toxic once the liver is too toxic to function properly. Once this occurs the workers bodily function will start to rapidly deteriorate.

The body does not have the capability to expel these fibers on its own. So they are there for the duration. The body is not designed to have foreign particles in it. Other particles consist of iron deposits and other metals including copper. Fibers are also part of the grinding disk.

Once you have a condition or disease you will own it. This disease will be yours and yours alone. You will have it until you get rid of it. Getting rid of your condition is not possible through today's medical establishment. Your family doctor can only provide Antibiotics. They will refer you to a specialist. The specialist can only provide antibiotics and surgery, all at your expense. You will see no relief. During this time the source of your disease remains deep into the dark crevasses of your body trapped there with no way out. Once you have arrived at this point you will have experienced extreme pain in the worst locations. Possibly having several diseases at the same time. Your daily dose of pain is 24/7. It will be a reminder to you till the day you die your stupidity for not knowing this information. Your pain is not just a discomfort it will be dreadful and will not stop. Possible a wheelchair bound.

Your extreme pain will become your prison. Your mind will scream for relief and no one can provide medical relief. Out of your pain will come desperation. In your desperation you will find a way. You will accept new ideas. Anything to make it go away. Perhaps full body cleanses.

Full body cleanses is the only way you can get long term relief. Once you start doing full body cleanses the disease causing agents can be expelled permanently. During this process there is a lot of discomfort. It is a daily ritual. You must be fully dedicated. You will learn a whole new life. But you will have hope. You can do this. It is your only, and I do mean only hope.

In this day and age in the year of our Lord of 2008. Medical coverage for many is non existent. 600,000 Oregonians alone have no coverage. The medical establishment is ineffective. All they are willing to do is manage your disease. You are truly alone.

Welders are a hard working people. They go from job to job trying to just earn a pay check. Companies are aware of these toxic conditions but it is not to their benefit to make it known to you. This creates a win-lose. They rake in record profits. You get a tiny paycheck, they lay you off. You go to the next job just in a little worse condition than when you started. They get off the hook and are not held responsible.

Welders get absolutely no respect. They work in a toxic trade in a toxic environment, often under extreme conditions. They literally break their backs trying to please their employer. Most often working without the right tools, or best yet with faulty equipment. They are yelled at, screamed at, threatened and harassed by their employers. Their employers are constantly holding their jobs hostage. A welder never feels any security. They are used and abused in every sense of the word. They are treated worse than dogs. They are like dogs at the dog pound. Then they are kicked to the curb by their employer at the first chance of opportunity. You show loyalty, while your employer shows you betrayal. In addition, many managers are anti civil. Their internal nature is clearly anti employee. Their internal guidance system is upside down, backwards, perverted, and twisted.

This report is meant to empower you at every way. Take this report with you every where you go and keep it in your tool box as part of your profession. Show it often, refer to it often. Together we can make a difference. Only through a matter of time can things change. Change is the reason for this report.

In retrospect, the compensation received is not enough. This welding trade is a diabolical trade. The pay needs to be much higher. Let's make a difference together. Take a step back and reevaluate it all. Count the cost. Then make a more informed decision.

By change I mean the money. It's all about the money. The amount you receive per hour. It is not a fair exchange of currency. It is lopsided to the company's favor. This tide must shift. No amount of money is worth the shit you have to put up with, the conditions you work in, the respect you never get, the hatred and double standards by managers and not to mention the many diseases you will receive for your many years of dedicated service to the welding industry. It is truly diabolic. It deserves the skull and cross bones symbol.

OVERCOMMING THE DISEASE

Overcoming this disease has been the most difficult thing that I have ever had to do. This is a true story as can be told by someone who has experienced these things. No fairy tales here bothers and sisters. This true story starts once upon a time long ago, back in the days of old. I went to a welding school in Tucson, AZ back in 1976. All they taught was stick welding a brazing as well as oxygen and acetylene welding. Some torch but not much. They did not teach very much but that is beside the point. This small was run by the state education program since I was in foster care. This is what I was eligible for.

This state run school is no longer in operation. I have no idea how long it remained but it was there in my time. Like all things they go through change. This was a six month to completion course.

Once I found work the fibers started accumulating. The trash build up was to begin. These toxic fibers started screwing with my body within a few years. Of course like all welders I went home ever night face full of black soot, very similar to a coal miner. This went on what seems like forever. I did not feel good until I went home dirty. This soot covered my face, nostrils and lungs. I always thought this trade one to be proud of. I couldn't see myself doing anything else. No matter where I worked I served my master well, always without complaint.

In the beginning the health equation one did not understand. I had great health. But over the years things began to subtly change. My body began feeling the signs. But being young I did not understand what it was or exactly or why. Day by dirty grinding things changed.

Over the thirty year span this trade changed my body dramatically and how I viewed the world. The long term toxic build up in my body came to a painful conclusion. My pain became so unbearable I was forced to take matters into my own hands. I had to take my health out of the doctor's eyesight. It was that or become disabled.

In the beginning history I worked in the truck building industry, Pressure vessel shops. I built cranes. Steel fabrication, water storage tanks lots of field work and then came sheet metal, steam pipe, rock crushers. Now there were lots of places in between. This is only a snapshot of where I have worked. After many years of working in the trade I tried my hand at wrought iron and metal sculptures. It came somewhat easy for me. I have a portfolio that is pretty good I think.

Over the years lots of toxicity built up accumulations in my body. Its devastation was starting to manifest itself in my male production area which is the prostate. My sperm began to appear stringy in appearance. It changed from white to brown. I began at the age of 45 to really take notice of this. I had no choice because it was becoming a painful condition coming on rapidly.

My emotions were also taking a hit. I was at this time very cynical in nature. I had a very bad attitude towards most everything. I was angry all the time. I had not yet realized what has happened to me because I was very busy in my life.

The toxic build up was now at its highest point of power. My body cannot take any more toxicity. I was at maximum capacity. I had become infested. I am in possession of a severe chronic prostate infection. But it was non cancerous. I was now introduced to severe pain. I also had a severe case of acid reflux. My kidney disease was nothing compared to these two bad ass conditions. I cannot say which one is more painful. They are both demons on the body. They bring upon hell itself. The acid reflux brings upon the person just as much suffering as the prostate condition. At this point my kidneys were at 57% capacity. This is considered kidney disease but at first I did not realize this as the doctors did not refer to it as such until later.

I did not arrive suddenly at this point. At first I attained a bladder infection to start things off. I had this taken care of until the symptoms arrive again. But this time it was not a bladder infection. It was something more cynical. My urination was painful and burned. My ejaculation was hurtful due to the infection of my maleness. It made relations with my wife at the time uneasy, both physically and psychologically. I had obtained a painful burning sensation between my legs. When I would walk I felt like there was broken glass between my thighs. My scrotum was very painful as well. There are three reasons for pain. Talk about misery. There was also the issue of acid reflux. I was trying to get off my medication at this time because it was weakening my bones. This alone produced untold misery. I had developed a wheezing at this time I instinctively knew that I have to stop doing this trade. I gave it up for a few years so I could heal. But at this time in my life I will never forget.

Out of this dark history of time brought a brand new way of looking at things. Out with the old and in with the new. I felt like the serpent has spewed me out. And a rebirth had begun.

By my writing this I am attempting to share this story with the world. For in fact it is strange. As we all know that fact is stranger than fiction. For what follows is a true story of my attempt to eradicate these conditions. By the way I now, in retrospect look at these conditions as demons in their own right.

MY DARK QUEST

    I had started on my quest for answers. In truth I was following my insights. All I had was an idea and a phone number. I had the phone number of the witches brew made by the hippy witch in the forest. I made the contact and then hopped on my fast pony and rode with gusto and destiny. As I rode across icy pathways I felt somewhat like the fallen angel that descended to earth in anger resentment. I rode as a lightning bolt to my destination. I was angry at everything mostly at my self. Nothing mattered except what is in front of me. I was angry at doctors, wife, job, myself, stupidity everywhere. My destiny held in the balance. My pain was a hindrance in all things. But this was a turning point. My pain became a guide. At this point I listened to all things that were brand new. This brand new language was called alternatives. I gave the doctors all my attention. They were bringing to me illusions and dead ends. They were in denial about things in their own way. I found them to be less than forthcoming. Their pills were a joke. I new that I must bypass their world! This is why I refer to this time as a dark quest. I had no one who could provide answers. In short I was entering the dark ages.

    There was not any one that I can turn to for right answers. I found each person and encounter along the way to be my teacher to become the whole. This is why I am writing this on paper. So that It can become something for somebody someday.

    In my personal world I was looked upon with deep suspicion. I found my self alone and isolated. No one including my spouse could arrive at this place that I now found myself, I had been separated. The only guidance I received was my intellect, intuition, guided by triple pain and confusion. It has isolated me to this day. The gods must have a reason.

    My search for answers first included my medical dictionary. I had an old one sitting around from the past. Daily I gave easily two to four hours of searching. I was desperate to find what was wrong with me. I searched seven days a week until I found answers. It did provide some but not what I had to have. I guess you could say that I had Welders disease. But there was no clear definition of this in the medical dictionary. But it gave mea little insight.

At about this time, I came into the knowledge of alkalized water that would be a great help but did not engage at this time. I came into contact with herbal remedies that I latched onto as though I was an infant latching onto the life giving breast. This was the turning point. The herbal remedies are a process that expanded to this very day. It is an ongoing process. It is a life style now.

The right fluids, the right foods, the right thoughts are all essential precursors for right feelings. This, of course, is where I lose most people. While they all agree in principle they still do not identify in a deep way. This is why I wrote the living dead.

As I rode that icy day upon the black pathways I felt the magical stir. I new that I could make magic happen. I was released from the past thinking and believed as I rode that there had to be a way other than the non way of doctors. I knew that the doctors were for the living dead. If I am to live then I had to stay away from them. I had to figure out the hidden answers. Any sympathy I received seemed to be false sympathy. Any concern seemed to feel like false concern. In short it was false reality. It is the world of the living dead.

As I arrive at my destination. I was received with the up-most compassion form the witch as she handed me her special brew. She provided some new insights as to new directions. At this time my eyes and being began seeing new things and out of this I had come to renewed beliefs. I sensed a deeper understanding and a deeper knowledge about the human body than the doctors, it is more earthy. This witches' brew was an herbal gasoline. A combination between a high racing fuel and strychnine. It striped the pain causing agents from the body. I later found out this concoction is called detox formula.

Its ingredients include: Red clover blossoms. Chaparral, Oregon Cayenne, Poke root, Lobelia seed &Golden seal root. In addition to this I learned about the colon cleans and other bodily cleanses. By passing through these remedy experiences I have arrived on another plain of thinking. I am in a state where few can identify. In retrospect, this was the right choice for me. I have found that not too many people will even consider these life giving alternatives. Their minds are of the living dead.

I did the detox and right away found some pain relief. My urinary pain had subsided within two days. I was dumfounded. The doctors antibiotics took thirty days to work, and then came back within one month. Shazaam! Then there was the prostate formula that was an excellent addition to the detox. It worked wonders as well. It was all down hill from here. I bought the kidney bladder cleanse, and the liver gallbladder cleanse from Dr Shultz. The rest is history.

SHOCK AND HORROR

What came out of my body I cannot really describe the details. It is shocking and unbelievable that the doctors will deny its existence. There came out of me during these cleanses infections, hair, and balls of fibers I think are morgellons. Along with iron particles and parasites. My computer does not even recognize the word morgellons. I learned about these little devils through a University Of Oregon graduate. Morgellons are a recent mystery that is occurring throughout the world that no one can either deny not explain. Go to www.morgellons.com for further explanation. I did not understand the full impact of what was happening. I did these cleanses several years ago as of this writing. I speak in view of the past. The way I see it today is 'what a shocking time'. You cannot explain this to people in any way. I now realize that my body was a junk yard. This sums it up nicely. I tell people this same thing.

I now pay closer attention what I pass into the urinal. You would not believe me if I told you to this day I pass things into the urinal almost daily.

After going through the herbal remedies and changing my diet for a time period not specified. I found that my pain had subsided greatly but not all together. I continued with the prostate cleanse and the detox. They worked wonders.

But I also had to change my diet because my acid reflux was still a lingering pain. I found a couple of things that worked wonders. I discovered Genesis today. 4total Calcium. Where the cows get their calcium. It is a pro-biotic calcium based liquid. This is the first thing that put my acid reflux down fast. I also discover spinach leaves. This helps greatly as well, any vegetable for that matter. Then there is good apples. I found this to be an excellent source of antacid. I have also found that over a period of a few years that this diet change has helped my over all health.

I took my activities all the way to the end. I did all I could for my self and then the time came to get professional help. I located a great nature-pathic doctor. This doctor was a she. So to explain my male problem with her did not prove to be an issue. I found great understanding here in this place. This practitioner took healing to another level. She used vibration therapy that vibrated more infection out of my body.

THE RESULT

The results were on going issues and still are to this day. Detox is also painful. My pain has subsided at least ninety percent in the prostate. My seminal; health has improved dramatically. There are still lots of progress to go. But hey! I have no more erectile dis-function. I have sexual health again.

I have pain in acid reflux but nothing like I had it before. I take no medications for it. I find myself unable to eat some foods because of the chemical make up of the product. After eating box foods and fast foods or anything un-fresh my body reacts like it has been poisoned. My kidneys that were at 57% have been calculated by my family doctor as having been raised to over 90%. My overall health is once again in the athletic range. I watch my diet and do eat that hamburger or pizza once in a while, but not too often though. I don't like being poisoned.

A CURSED MAN

Talk about being a curse! This blessing came with a curse. I am no longer welcome on my job. In fact they fired me. I lost my marriage. My wife divorced me. I lost contact with my kids because I am no longer welcome. I lost all that I had gained over a fifteen year period. I am looked at as though I am a threat to my in-laws. They react to me with extreme anger over I don't know what. They pretend me to be a bad Johnny when in fact I am a survivor. But it is ok because they were a disease and had to be expelled as well. While I was at dispelling these conditions I went on a campaign to expel my mind disease with it. Then I determined to rid my personal life of the disease therein as well. So I pulled the subconscious plug and drained it. To this day I can see there backward ways. They are filthy, nasty, lost and sick themselves unhappy. I am at a point that I shall pity the fools. Even people in my public life have put me off in the distance. Like they don't want to know me any more. I am no longer one of them they say. I can see their curse as well. I see their unhappiness stronger now.

THE BLESSING

The blessings are ever so subtle. I have no more old problems. I have new ones. But the new ones are different, like for instance writing this memo. I hope someone reads this and helps at least one person. I have become better at seeing things more clearly. I have great dreams. I have a lot more happiness. I have better overall health. But remember I had to fight for it. My mind and spirit have been taken to another plain of thinking. What must become of me now? Shake off the old and put on the new. I am now is search of others like myself. I seek other survivors that are like minded. Are you one of these rare people? If so, then we should talk. Let's walk into the future and create something new.

WHAT IS YOUR ASS WORTH

THE AMERICAN BITCH

What inspires me to write this is the fact the way female has treated me all of my life. As much as I have tried to communicate with them in public and in private I am always infuriated by their lack of respect towards me. I am a well respected individual. I have a normal personality like any human. But there is just something about female that is nothing but out right stinks. Women all the time fuck me off no matter how clean my thinking may be. No matter what is it that I become women will not consider me a human being worth knowing. This really started as a small child But that material is another book for a later time and place.

Right now I will attempt to concentrate on this issue as tightly as possible. My back ground is broad which means from the church to the streets. I have wide scope views.

Let's start this off by stating that the worst kind of women that I see out in America is not the hooker or the neighborhood he/she. The worst women are the cold calculating long term criminal.

She starts out as your sweet heart in high school. Since child hood she sees her opportunities in her family settings. She takes notice how the game is played because of Mommy. Mommy has taken daddy for a hard ride. She saw mommy take daddy's house, car and too his children away as well. Mommy has the power to dictate to the system all she wants and she gets it at the man's expense.

Mean while the man is left out in the cold working two jobs and having to pay her all his hard earned wages and support his ex family for the long duration while he barely gets by. Some men don't make it through this period. They whither and die or end up in jail.

Women have been granted the power to bring down the most powerful man in the universe, that being the President of the United States. While she only being only an intern. This is insidious. This is really a joke.

Let me reverse this. If the woman was the most powerful person in the universe and she had an affair with the opposite sex, would she be brought down from her position by a lowly intern? Of course not. My point exactly. So why do we have women exercising power over men in this society when it is so lopsided. Women cry about everything. They cry because their hair is the wrong color, they cry because they broke a nail. They cry and belly ache and bitch and nag us to death. Our system has given them the power against our will. I believe women have been given this power because it helps keep in check the men in our society by bringing things against him. I have had nothing but problems with women since I was a born baby. I am sick and tired of American women walking about in this society thinking they are queens and continually reduce men to nothing. I do not see any virtue in women anywhere. I do not see sweetness any where either. I do not see helpfulness. I have rarely seen ever throughout my entire life anything good from women that would warrant pity. Women in my life have all been ruthless bitches. This includes my mother. I might as well include your mother as well.

I have graduated to the point that I now view prostitutes a better option as the American housewife. I just cannot muster any respect for the American woman anymore.

How about an example here? There was this mighty body builder. He was very famous. He was very power in body. He has to have a very power mind to shape his body. This blessed man went on to create great movies and show the world his great body. He gave us great joy. He became so popular that the State of California made him Governor. He was voted in by the public and was found a winner. There was a wonderful woman that caught his eye. She wanted child. He gave her one. He brought forth life and an heir to his fortunes. Can't see anything wrong there. Now his wife takes all of his money, his house and his possessions. She calls him bad names. She accuses him of mismanagement of marriage. Then she sues him. Now ask your self is this love? I don't think so.

Instead of loving this mighty man and being grateful for all this man has done for her what does this wife end up doing? She takes him for hundreds of millions of dollars. What is his crime? His only crime has been nothing really except to do that which was natural. He is in obedience to his instincts.

She manipulated events with the hand of the master. Then sits back and claims innocence. This is the same tactic all women use covertly in all relationships that go sour. She obviously wanted it to go bad. She created her own circumstances through non cooperation and or cooperation.

Now let's look at this in reverse. She could not satisfy this powerful man. She failed him in the bedroom. She held back knowing he would look else where. She manipulated these circumstances. She is responsible for her own marriage. She could not meet his needs. She was angry inside about something. Perhaps jealousy was her motivation. She intuitively knew that he deserved better and silently sent those vibrations forth and he responded. This makes her insecurity the very core of these events. This is why he looked else where. This is why events unfolded as they did.

Besides, no man should not have to stay true to any woman. It is not in his nature to do so. A man's nature is that he looks to every woman to meet his one need. A woman's nature is to look to the one man to fit her every need. The only true way to capture a great man is through satisfaction. There is no other way.

She clearly did not keep this in mind as her every whim was taken care of. She had no reason not to satisfy her man. She was to important in life to pay attention to the one thing she holds dear, Her marriage. Did she care enough?

Excuse me I don't think so. I do not know the details about this couples life. But I don't see her being virtuous either. Like every powerful mans woman she will steal away his soul if you let her.

Women don't have what it takes to just walk away. Hell! They don't even have what it takes to satisfy a man in the bed room. This is the very fucking reason for all the divorces in this country. Don't think so. Ok smarty! Tell me why did you get divorced? If your woman was the slut you wanted her to be would you still be married to her? That is the test. If a woman can out fuck the man then she can perform. All women can out fuck a man. The answer to all marriages is all out fucking sex.

A man is simple. A woman is complicated. So we have complication ruling over the simple. You get my drift here. We have the woman acting like her pussy is made of gold. She protects and uses it like a weapon and yet it bleeds. I am sure this is a natural tendency. But we have got to have a different standard from here forward.

I think it is now time for woman to step up to true equanimity. Take nothing that you did not earn. We men have supported these bitches all of our lives. It is time to stop. They just live with you because they can screw you over some later date. Women are abusive in every sense of the word. I have seen it all of my 52 born years.

The worst of all women are not hookers. Hell, at least we know what to expect from these women. They get to business then they go. No problem. It is the American house wife that is screwing up everything.

MOMMY AS TEACHER

Since childhood a little girl dreams of growing up and having a family. She plays with her dolls' she dresses them and dreams of one day of having her own family. Mean while reality around her is playing out like a retard on fire. Mommy and daddy are going through their PMS, Post Martial Situation. It plays out to its end. She sees all this. Now she gets married and does the same thing. This never ends. It will play out into the next generation. But in the mean time she thinks things over and comes up with a five step plan and then goes on and finds a stupid sucker to implement her criminal ways.

There is fantasy then there is reality. Today's little children are learning early on who has the power. She has fantasies of house playing and being a mother then it gets peppered with the reality. Together they blend and we get the results. You know the story from here.

But she has got to survive. So she picks her target. She pushes for marriage. Of course she has to have two or three kids. Well, we have to have a house to live in too you know. You know we need two cars and all the things in the house that make a house a home. It all sounds right. It is all calculated But now she has you hooked. The man has made all things happen. Now she has everything. She has now decided to play the nasty house wife. She starts nagging. She complains about everything. This is her way of starting to push the man out the door. This is the woman's way of ending the relationship. She can't come out and just say I am tired of this relationship. She goes about it by nagging and pretending to be upset about her man in everything he does. Even if the man placates her the chances go down but every little. Chances are almost one hundred percent it will end in divorce. This is her pushing things to their limit. This is the man's clue to take her to the bedroom and stick his dick in her ass. Give her a mean fucking. But most men don't because they are repelled by this bitch. I say fuck her anyway.

Woe-man

Once a woman starts complaining and constantly nagging this is her way of bringing the relationship to its conclusion. In other words they are precursors to the divorce. Nagging is the number one thing a man hates. Guess what they will do to initiate the end of the relationship? You guessed it, nagging. Nagging is defined as: scold or urge continually. To be persistently annoying. This is unnatural to our living organism.

During this time do you think that she knows not what she is doing? Not a chance in hell brother. She knows exactly what she is doing. You are just to stupid to see it. Brothers, I challenge you to just take a good look around you and see all the other people around you going through the exact same thing. Every thing I am telling you is right before your eyes. The only reason I can see it is because I was taken into hell and back for over 52 years. This is why I am writing this essay. I consider this essay a public warning to all men in dire need for clarification. This is an epidemic.

Once the man signs the marriage vows he has put his signature to his death sentence. These are ruthless bitches that are trained by dear mommy. This same dear mommy did not teach you her son how to deal with these bitches now did she? I don't think so. The reason is simple she has to mislead you to keep her secret to her self. She has trained you her dear male child to always bring the women flowers. Well this is very nice on the one hand but I say mommy what about these bitches. She just stands back and lets the bitches get their way too. She has now become the protector of the bitches.

I think there is inherent in most every female a strong hatred for men. This is why women are bitches. A woman has no loyalty except to her child. She will rule over man mercilessly in every way possibly for no good reason except to full fill her criminality. Just to exercise her power over him and make him feel hatred for her.

This is women's power. It is subtle and deadly. It is malicious, hateful, extremely selfish, and depressed. She is the destroyer of families. She destroys households. In addition to these nasty attributes I have witnessed women absolutely filthy and hideous to live with. Did I mention disgusting? Never in my life have I had the opportunity to dwell with female that was not filthy, nasty and just household hideous. I know that they are not all like that but I swear I have never known one that was clean.

Now that the little girl has lived out her dream and got the house, the car, and the kids not to mention the man on the criminal list. She has made a criminal out of her husband. She now teaches her girls how to do the same thing.

This is America's most dangerous thing for man. The most dangerous weapon in the house is not the man's pistol. It's his god damn bitch. Woe to this man who has such a bitch.

The latest American rage for women is the past time of making a criminal out of their man. They find ways to make this happen. If a man walks up right he may still be taken unaware. The cunning of the bitch is powerful and creative. She will find a reason to put charges on her man even it she has to lie about it. Don't think so brother. I say to you, you have not been to the county lock up. Half the people in there are on domestic violence or drugs. I have seen so many men in the county on domestic charges that their head is spinning. Most don't understand how it got that way. I too was one of them. This is why I know. The bitch that did this to me is dead today, probably due to suicide, but dead nevertheless.

This story I am demonstrating here is all legal tender. But that is beside the point. Women have been screaming for equal rights. I say sure you have equal rights. I'm down for all that. This includes earning your own way, earning your own money. Now it will also include this report that will outline a new age woman. This old class of women is the criminal mind set. Time has come for things to be reversed. Flip the coin so to speak.

NEW AMERICAN BITCH

PROSTITUTION

For me to understand these women I am forced to put them into the classification of prostitute. I have tried to tell my self they these females are ladies and lovely God creatures. But every God damn one of them has proven me God damn wrong. Today's American bitches make the prostitute look like girl scouts.

Today's American bitches are no longer worthy of marriage. They use the marriage to steal a man's life from him. They usurp his riches. They do this by the man's signature. It is part of their five step plan. Now get this my brothers you never wanted marriage in the first place now did you? See what I mean? You were on the right path in the beginning. But she talked you into it and I could even bet she used her pussy to get her way. She will even go as far as to use the relationship with you as a weapon. Either marry me or I go find another sucker is her game. This is not love. This is targeting. This is the criminal mind set she is using. But since all of life is in slow motion we men don't pick up on it. She is entrapping and setting up for the kill at a later date.

Prostitution is not a professional occupation. It is a trade. Professional indicates something learned through higher learning. Prostitution is a layman's trade. As a layman they should receive layman's wages. This constitutes 10.00 to 20.00 dollars per hour. No more. Her pussy is not made of gold. They are flesh and blood and their pussy bleeds.

During intercourse the woman receives pleasure just as her male counterpart. This is why she has sex. Now to get one hundred dollars for this act on top of that while that male loses one hundred dollars is lopsided. While this is accepted practice the world over. I think a new a better way for the man is in order. A wife for hire and business partner combination. An all around woman. Fuck the bullshit.

Women and money are synonymous. We know this to be a fact. Then men use your money to get these bitches to do what you want. Women should be reduced to her new status. Reduced to zero. Let us start reducing women down to the nothing that they have done us men. Shake them down.

A worker makes minimum wage. They only make a few hundred dollars a week. A NWOP, NEW WORLD ORDER PROSTITUTE, should be nothing better.

Before I go any further let me break rank for a second and reverse this thinking. To have the right partner is to have an asset. To have the wrong partner is a detriment. I am not against any body here. I just think that we need to put things under the microscope and examine it from another view. I am a little harsh here. But I am also realistic. I personally will implement these new strategies my self after writing this essay. I will not be taken any longer. I am stretching this concept beyond its proper bounds because in the long run it will equal out in its own way. So I am stretching farther than it will realistically go.

Now where were we? Oh yes the bitch. In every woman there are two distinct personalities. There is the lovely lady then there is the bitch. These two personalities are opposite one another. I will not get deeper into these at this time. But you get my point. Since these ladies like conjuring the bitch inside then let us men treat them as such. Bitches!

If you choose to be a bitch with me then I will certainly accommodate you. I will take you as you are presenting yourself. If you act like a bitch then I will believe you to be a bitch.

The bitch mode: A woman goes into bitch mode and considers it a time management tool. While this is understandable on the one hand it is completely unnecessary to be this way to me. Not all women all the time. All women all the time are in the bitch mode. I even see it in the women in the church. No female is immune in this targeting. I am targeting all American Women. I am not alone in this assessment. Many American men are tired of American women. Being in the bitch mode may have its advantages up front but it has its drawback as well. It comes with a reversal of fortunes.

Stingy: Stingy meaning simply not generous. When it comes to giving credit to a man for his efforts she is outrageously stingy. She will not grant to her man any points for his hard work. A man will go to work and bring home the bacon thinking all things are right. Not so with the bitch. She gives him scant credit for his bringing home the bacon efforts. She sees things differently. She thinks it selfish of him to spend all his time at work. She shows herself unappreciative of this man's efforts. There are many more things to point out on this issue but I will stop hare. You get my point though.

Since women break up our relationships, because they take our kids away from us, take our houses, our cars and our wages then we will assign them to new world duties starting now. They have held us men hostage for far too long. They have earned the right to be reduced down to their own level They are little more than animal. They are representations from hell itself. Bitches are from hell!

In my life this is how I will treat them. They will satisfy me fully. I will learn to take my power back. I will not give it to them ever again. I will judge them by these new standards. What is your ass really worth? I will judge you as though you are a whore from hell until you prove me wrong.

1. Are she married? The idea here is she a game player? If you have had too many marriages then you are someone others cannot get along with. The longer you have been married the better. The less marriages the better. This shows cooperation. 5yrs or more 5pts, 4yrs or more 4pts, 3yrs or more 3pts, 2yrs or more 2 pts, 1yr or less 1pt.
2. How many failed relationships have you gone through? The idea here is you cannot seem to get along with other people. 5 or more 0 pts, 4 or more 1 pt, 3 or more 2 pts, 2 or more 3pts, 1 or more 4 pts.
3. Is she a bitch? Is she a cunt? Is she a lady? Is she a man hater? Is she a babe? You will know when you met her. Lady's , darlings, and babes are better. Babe/Lady 5 pts, darling 4 pts, great lover 3pts, bitch 2pts. Scrapper 1 pt, bitch/cunt 0 pts.
4. Does she do drugs and alcohol? What does she abuse? Crank and needle pushers are the worst. They are strongly associated with lying, stealing and bad trouble follows them everywhere. Next is cocaine. Cocaine is strongly associated with sex and pleasure. Marijuana should not even be mentioned, it is not a drug. It is a plus actually. But of course if she does not use anything is far better. Women are naturally complicated.

No drugs 5 pts, Marijuana only 4 pts, cocaine 3 pts, snorts 2 pts, needles, 1 pt. if she does needles and has fore on the body 0 pts.
5. Does she smoke tobacco and drink alcohol? The more of these two she does the worse it is. Women are naturally complicated drugs and alcohol make things worse. Besides they stink to high heaven. Yes is 0 pts, no is 1 pt.
6. Is she sickly? This is a clear indication as to how she takes care of her body. If she cannot take care of her own body then she cannot care anything about yours. Chances are she also cannot properly take care of her children's health as well. Takes no medications and is athletic 5 pts, athletic and 1 medication 4 pts, two or more medications 3 pts, Mental medications 2 pts, 3 or more medications 1 pt. 3 medications and mental 0 pts.
7. Does her pussy stink? Does her body smell? Does she have sores all over her face? Does she have needle tracks? If she has any of these symptoms then she gets no credit. Does she smell fresh Is highly preferred. Fresh 3 pts, acceptable 2 pts, strong body order but passable 1 pt, Bad body order and stinky pussy o pts.
8. Does she have kids? If she has kids then she is damaged goods. 0 kids 5 pts, 1 kid 4 pts, 2 kids 3 pts, 3 kids 2 pts, 4 kids 1 pt, 5 or more 0 pts.
9. Why is she seeking money for sex? To pay bills and feed the kids connotes responsibility. This is better than doing it for drugs.
Feed kids & pay bills 2 pts drugs and kids 1 pt, drugs only 0 pts.
10. What is her attitude? Does she have this god damn attitude? Or This sweet attitude? Loving attitude 4 pts, cooperative 3 pts, edgy 3 pts, depression 2 pts, bitchy 1 pt. any combination of the last three 0 pts.
11. Is she in school? Is she actively involved in learning in any capacity? If not this is undesirable. 4 yrs in

school 5 pts, 2 yrs 3 pts, just starting school 2 pts, no school 1 pt, uneducated 0 pts.
12. Is she employed? Is she employable? If not then this is undesirable. The idea here is she a responsible individual. You have to be tolerable to be employed. If employed 4 pts, if unemployed but employable 3 pts, if not employable 2 pts, if never employed 1 pt, depressed and needle users with depression 0 pts.
13. How old is she. The younger the better. The older the less valuable. The reason is simple. Men only want one thing. They want a girl stupid enough to sleep with him. Nothing more. 16-18 5 pts, 18-24 4 pts, 24-30 3 pts, 30-36 2 pts, 36-42 1 pt. 42-50 0 pts.
14. Do her tits sag? Sagging looks bad. Defying gravity is better. Tits sagging indicates unhealthy 0 pts, fake tits 1 pt, normal tits 2 pts, defy gravity naturally 3 pts.
15. Fat to body ratio. Nothing turns men off more than fat. A man of quality hates fat women. Athletic is most desirable. Athletic 4 pts, slim 3 pts, normal; 2 pts, over weight 1 pt, sloppy fat 0 pts.
16. How does she dress? Her dress indicates how she looks at her self on the inside. The higher the quality the better. The more sophisticated the more desirable. I personally prefer the business type dress. This speaks volumes. Classy 4 points, sexy 3 pts, average 2 pts, slutty 1 pt, trashy 0 pts.
17. Why is she tricking her self? Her stated reasons must connote responsibility as well as pleasure. Wife for hire 4 pts, business 3 pts, family 2 pts, personal 1 pts, drugs 0 pts.
18. What is her price? Women want a man's weekly wages for one night of sex. This is simply unacceptable. All for one or one for all. All of your money for one shot. Or all night for that which is reasonable. Good business is always win-win. All night reasonable working mans rates 2 pts. ($15.00 hr.) unreasonable

rates 1 pt, outrageous rates 0 pts.

BUSINESS WOMEN PROSTITUTES

Tomorrow's wife will be a paid prostitute. She will be paid a weekly amount and she will perform to her man's standards and earn it the same way she has to earn a paycheck. She will be in tune to business and dedicated to this end. There will be no more giving away your paycheck to this bitch and she does all things that will make your life absolutely miserable. There will be no more of this mystical mind set. This is double payment. This is doing time. It is extremely unwise, and a total waste of our most precious asset, our time. To get the most out of a relation ship it must be wiped clean of all bull shit. Business and pleasure together in one package. Its all about the money. Better yet it's all about the harmony and being on the same path. A mutually satisfying beneficial path. Doing it together is better than doing it alone. Two minds generate the power of three. She needs you and you need her.

If you are going to spend your life and money with someone and they not perform then they should be kicked to the curb. This is exactly the way women have done to you and me. Although covertly. Except they used unreasonable tactics. Their tactics are mystical and totally unreasonable non understandable, and totally unexplainable. Time to reverse this trend.

Another reason for this essay is this. Women are more demanding than a dog and cat combined. They are more unreasonable than a whole farm of animals. They are the most stressful creatures known to man. They are actually more stressful than the job. It is said that arguing with a woman is just as stressful as defusing a bomb.

This point system is based upon the one they secretly have. Their secret point system is not only stingy but it is starving men of their right place in the relationship. This must be the reason the Bible states that women are forbidden by God to exercise power over a man. Yet, again women cannot accept this statement. Any woman that cannot accept this statement is in fact sexist. 99% of women are sexist. Let us all men put them back where they belong.

They walk around as though they are supreme creatures and full of power. The real fact of the matter is that they are inferior. This is the reason why the Scriptures make this statement. Woman is subject to man because it is from the man that she came from. Not the other way around. I am not into abuse of any kind here. I'm just looking for equality.

QUEEN STATUS

Women can be the queen if they really want it. Today's man wants you to become the prostitute of his dreams. This is the very reason his eyes roam outside the relationship. He is looking for the sleazy slut to make his fantasy come true. A man wants the whole woman. He wants her ass as well.

The ideal woman is this: a great cook in the kitchen, and clean maid in the house. A slut and a prostitute in the bedroom. Men want nothing more than this. This is giving all. If you cannot be all that a man needs he should kick your ass to highway along with your kids as well. You can go find some other fool to take care of your stupid ass. Their will always be another fool.

The new world order queen of the house swallows. Takes it in the ass and is totally willing to keep her man drained of sap. By doing this you will have all the sex you want in return. Then your reward will be an undivided household. One where there is no strife. Your mystical mind set will be put to rest. This is the new queen. So can you claim queen status ladies? You have nothing to be proud of until you do. Only through queen status can you ask anything of men. Give your all to get all.

Men let's employ these new strategies in this new age. The power of this strategy is based on the fact all energy generated in the humans are just that energy. All energy is channeled to the sexual side of nature. Channel all energy to this end and things will only get better. But not perfect.

I will also say this one last thing before I sign off. Once a woman starts to prostitute herself she automatically steps into Sheol. She has her feet in Sheol. This is hell. Because she has her feet in Sheol she will devalue all things. Perhaps this is why she already does. This explains why women are nothing but hell.
WRITTEN BY:
ERNEST JOHNSON

About the Author

Dear Reader,

    My name is Ernest Johnson. If this letter reaches your eyes and ears, then pay attention to the details. Our galaxy is fully occupied by the unseen gods. All of them are positioning themselves to bring about the Judgment of End Times. All heavenly forces and wicked forces have their agenda. They are all active. They all have hardened positions and winner takes all. Where we are at on the great apocalypse time clock is alarming to say the least. I speak to all conscious beings, both dead and alive, to support anyone, anywhere who can bring you deep knowledge that will enlighten our understanding on the unforeseen forces.

Deeply you know this subject I'm speaking of. You instinctively understand what is at stake. You know you heart beats to your dream. To be faceless is to be enlightened. Give up self to allow the energy of these forces to lead you to your destiny, whatever it is, for only you decide.

I have been from heaven to hell to bring to you the nasty facts of life. BS/No BS razor's edge, set on fire by the Holy Spirit. I can only be your friend by not becoming your friend. My material is not the light hearted. You may not be suited for my writings.

Duality is misleading if we judge from this place. Church is not what it seems. Hell is neither Christ or Satan! Truth is, your reality is only that, your own reality. I have brought to you Earth shattering, thunder thinking. You will learn by subjecting yourself to this new cutting edge, bone shattering thunder. Only then can you appreciate the spirit of man.

If you think this letter is either honest or deceptive, you are right either way. But do us both a favor, reread this letter. Act with love or hatred. Either one will work. Just educate yourself in any way you choose. But learn, you must do. We live in a world that doesn't understand deep inner things. But we all crave it. My material is my best that this hard-working man of iron can muster. Honesty and truth are not the same. The church is not what is seems. My material is designed to clear all the cobwebs, address the sin of man from a dual mind set, with quadruple points of view.

This is why nothing is as it seems. Learn why you're here. What your mission is. What your part is. Last but not least, where you'll end up.

This is how I present my audio. It's shut up, sit your ass down and listen to what the gods have to say to you. Period! But not all at once. Each subject is just that, one subject. But all combined, Yes! After continuing for a season you will understand this to be true!

Stand for something or fall for anything! The cosmic gates are about to swing wide. Support for this cause is paramount. Capture the energy, capture the matter. Live life on the run!

Whatever it is that you desire, first rule is to lock yourself into the energy of it. Look deeply into the subject and dive in. That's it. Secret revealed! All success is wrapped up in this key!
Ernest Johnson

www.ingramcontent.com/pod-product-compliance
Lightning Source LLC
Chambersburg PA
CBHW032049090426
42744CB00004B/138